Journal of
Melanie Klein and Object Relations

An International Journal Devoted to the Understanding of Object Relations

VOLUME 15, NUMBER 1, MARCH 1997

esf PUBLISHERS

BINGHAMTON & CLUJ

JOURNAL OF MELANIE KLEIN AND OBJECT RELATIONS is a quarterly published in March, June, September and December of each year by *esf* Publishers, Binghamton, NY, USA.

THE ANNUAL SUBSCRIPTION RATE for four issues is $60.00 (Canada and US) for individuals, and $100.00 (Canada and US) for institutions. All orders outside Canada and US, add $24.00 postage. Back and current issues are available at $20.00 per issue (orders outside Canada and US add $6.00 postage). *When subscribing, indicate whether you desire to start with the current issue or the current volume.* All prices quoted in US dollars. All payments should be made by check or money order through a US bank. Payments from outside the United States should be made by international money order in US funds. When ordering from Canada and paying by check, please write on your check "Pay in US funds." Subscriptions and address changes should be sent directly to: *esf* Publishers, 1 Marine Midland Plaza, East Tower– Fourth Floor, Binghamton, NY 13901, USA.

BOOKS, PERIODICALS AND ADVERTISING INQUIRIES should be sent directly to the publisher: 1 Marine Midland Plaza, East Tower–Fourth Floor, Binghamton, NY 13901, USA. All books and materials received will be listed under BOOKS RECEIVED and ARTICLES NOTICED. All advertisement should conform to the standards of the journal and its publisher. Advertisement guidelines and rates are available upon request.

JOURNAL OF MELANIE KLEIN AND OBJECT RELATIONS is included in the PsychINFO system. For reference purposes, use the abbreviation *J. M. Klein Obj. Rel.*

Effective with Volume 14, Number 2, the journal is printed on acid-free paper. The paper used in this publication mets the minimum requirements of the American National Standards for Information Sciences—Permanence of Paper for Printed Library Materials, ANSI Z39.48-1984. ∞

Cover photo: Dr. W.C.M. Scott in his office (1982 or 1983). All photographs courtesy of Dr. Patrick Mahony.

ISBN 1-883881-22-6
Manufactured in the United States of America

Suggestions, Criticism?

It is your journal. Let us know how we are doing. . .

Tel.: (607) 772-4966   Fax: (607) 723-1401

IN MEMORIAM

DR. W. CLIFFORD M. SCOTT (1903-1997)

It was learned that Dr. W. Clifford M. Scott died on Sunday, January 19th 1997, at the age of 93 after a brief illness.

Dr. Scott was a founding member of the Canadian Psychoanalytic Society and Institute, as well as a former President of the British Psycho-Analytic Society.

As the following monograph by Dr. Patrick Mahony demonstrates, Dr. Scott was a prolific writer and a highly personal thinker, as well as an endlessly inspiring teacher for the many who like himself learned to value his originality and creativity.

At a personal level over more than thirty years, I was privileged to enjoy his zest for life as well as his warmth and generosity, as a mentor and close personal friend.

Dr. Scott will be celebrated and remembered as having been his own man and a man for all seasons.

Paul Lefebvre, M.D., Member,
Canadian Psychoanalytic Society and Institute

In Montreal, on the 19th of January 1997, died W. Clifford M. Scott, M.D., in the ninety-fourth year of his youth.

He had been a practicing psychoanalyst for over sixty years, and he will be remembered by his friends, colleagues and students as well as by the whole psychoanalytic world for his numerous papers, particularly on depression and mania, sleep, dreams and the body image.

With his kaleidoscopic mind, he was forever seeing new aspects of things and pushing further ahead the limits of psychoanalysis. He was particularly dedicated to the world of publication, as a writer and as an editor of numerous journals. He was constantly encouraging analysts to write about their new ideas: "Why don't you write a paper about it, just a page, or even a paragraph." My regrets, respect and admiration are included in this paragraph.

Monique Meloche
Société Psychanalytique de Montreal

Dr. W.C.M. Scott in his office (1982 or 1983)

An Introduction to Clifford Scott: His Theory, Technique, Manner of Thinking and Self-Expression

Patrick J. Mahony

Virtually a piece of psychiatric and psychoanalytic history, Clifford Scott has had more than 60 years of clinical experience and close professional relationships with many of the leading psychiatrists and analysts of this century. Scott merits a study in terms of his theory, technique, manner of thinking and self-expression. Key themes in his broad-ranging theory are the dormancy triangle and dreaming. Scott's technique is sui generis. Primary process elements both enhance his manner of thinking as self-expression as well as often render them difficult to understand upon first reception.

KEY WORDS: Primary narcissism; Oceanic bliss; Catastrophic chaos; Dormancy triangle; Going to sleep; Sleep; Sleepiness; Waking; Dreaming; Residue; Memory; Anticipation; Oscillation; Maximilization; Minimalization; Recursivity; and Scotsland.

By virtue of more than 60 years of clinical experience and his close professional relationships with many of the leading psychiatrists and analysts of this century, Scott is a piece of psychiatric and psychoanalytic history. He studied under Paul Schilder and Adolf Meyer, the most influential North American psychiatrist in our time. He became Melanie Klein's first analytic candidate in analysis, and was one of the pioneering few who began to analyze schizophrenic and manic-depressive patients on a regular basis. He had supervision with Klein herself, with Ernest Jones, and with Ella Sharpe. Scott analyzed Winnicott for one session and both of Winnicott's second wives for a number of years. And he himself supervised a host of notable analysts, including Masud Khan. Finally, he was *a* if not *the* principal figure who established psychoanalysis in Canada.

Scott has further historical distinctiveness. I know of no one, from Freud to Winnicott and up to the present day, who has left such a unique record of having treated so many different kinds of fascinating and sometimes strange patients. And within that overall unique record some of the individ-

JOURNAL OF MELANIE KLEIN AND OBJECT RELATIONS, 1997, 15(1), 5-50 ual cases themselves are unique within the annals of psychoanalytic treat-ment. That record stands as a testimony of Scott's "long sitting" wakeful concern about strange clinical phenomena. He observed them, analyzed them, and had enough wonder left over to write them up for us. Perusing that record, as we shall do, is like a visit to "Scotsland".

Even a cursory examination of Scott's writings and conferences will reveal his omnivorous reading as well as his abounding interests in many fields, from the pure and social sciences to all the arts. Bearing in mind Scott's proposal that we take all that Freud told us as one big dream (Scott, 1986c),[1] the educated lay reader may further enjoy the minuteness of Scott's perceptual observations and his constant attention given to initial appear-ances of clinical phenomena. And the analytic reader in particular will experience the evidence of a relatively new kind of clinical management which is worthy of the eponymous adjective Scottsian.

In Scott's clinical theory we recurrently come upon five basic thematic subjects: instincts, primary narcissism and states, the body image, the ego's development in the pain-pleasure interaction, and the sleeping and dream-ing dynamic. For Scott, instinct and drive are without difference in the beginning (Scott, 1987b). Contrary to Klein, he believes that aggression is reactive, not primary, and that the death instinct is a disorganization of what is inherited (Hunter, 1995, pp. 196-197). Considering the other end of the life cycle, Scott agrees with Flugel about the need to look for evidence of new instinctive behavior in the senescent dying person; but whereas Flugel stresses the difficulty of clinically showing that the earliest kind of aggres-sion is self-aggression, Scott suggests that it would be more profitable to look for early oscillating behavior producing inactivity (Scott, 1953a).

Scott's other major difference with Klein concerns primary narcissism: whereas she felt that object relation is there from the beginning, he feels that initially there is a primary narcissism before object relations (Hunter, 1995, pp. 196-197). Primary narcissism is either oceanic bliss or what Scott has called catastrophic chaos; in those states are found much consciousness and movement; a confusion between phantasy, perception, memory, action, and anticipation; but no stable boundaries, no insides and outsides, no me, and not me (Scott, 1978b; 1982, p. 152). Both states of primary narcissism can be returned to in partial or total regression (Scott, 1985).

Scott also situates the later primary states of patients in terms of the two archaic polar states: an oceanic bliss, such as in orgastic and creative moments, in which all time and space are one and all affects flow into one good feeling; and catastrophic chaos, such as in depressive nihilism, panic attacks and paranoid crises, in which the universe, our body and its contents are fragmented, and the overall affect is that of hate, distress, despair, and fear (Scott, 1975c, p. 341). In contrast to much contemporary emphasis on the pleasure and pain in the polar cosmic and chaotic states, Scott has found the factor of boundlessness more important (Scott, 1975c, pp. 340-341).

Klein described at length how the disillusionment of primary narcissism is followed by the paranoid-schizoid position. Scott (1985) faulted Klein, however, for the neglect of time within her spatially biased conception of object relations and splittings—thus, for example, he urges the integration of Klein's notion of part and whole objects with the relationship of present newness, the memory of the past and the anticipation of the future. Likewise, Scott disputes Freud's hypothesis that the first split into good-inside and bad-outside takes place concurrently rather than sequentially. Also, relevant also here is Scott's (1978a) theory that ego development occurs in tandem with the capacity of making discriminations: the discrimination of hallucination being first, followed by that of sensation, phantastic image, and memory image.

Scott's (1985) theory centrally involves the corporeal schema succeeding primary narcissism. The child's body schema includes a temporal complexity about his past, present, and future; it also refers to that conscious or unconscious integrate of sensations, perceptions, conceptions, affects, memories and images of the body from its surface to its depths, and from its surface to the limits of space (Scott, 1948b, pp. 142-143; cf. 1985). If the ego arises from corporeal sensations coming principally from the surface of the body, it rather early becomes an introjection from this surface. A new splitting between the boundary of the body and what is "projected into the interior" gives rise to the psychic apparatus (Scott, 1985, p. 29). Boundaries, it follows, also include depth. Still, we must recognize that Freud's designation of the ego as a mental projection from the surface of the body is a metapsychological formulation of the earliest splitting, for the mind does not exist as an entity (Scott, 1948b, p. 152).

Alongside zonal development, the ego unfolds through an overall pleasure-pain dynamic occurring in five stages and marked by various regressive, progressive, and oscillating tendencies. To simplify radically: early on, the child lives in a preambivalent (Scott, 1964a, p. 374) cosmic bliss and catastrophic chaos, attended by splitting and confusion that affect megalomania and persecutory feelings. From this organized or disorganized narcissistic oneness occurs a progression to many kinds of ambivalence, involving two affects, and multivalence involving more than two affects. The progression continues on to sadomasochism; then a capacity to bear or inflict pain without being sadomasochistic; next, a working through a manic state of denial, envy and admiration; and finally, a zest for reparation of past damage and an anticipatory openness to new objects and opportunities (Scott, 1981b, pp. 1-4; 1986a, p. 8; 1988, pp. 130-131) so that one may "risk even greater losses by loving to live more intensely" (Scott, 1986a, p. 9).

Figure 1. W.C.M. Scott at Bad Wilbad, Summer of 1932,
during his analysis with Mrs. Klein

"He stayed at Bad Wilbad and every day took the Berghan from the valley to the top of Sommerberg for a two-hour session in her hotel room" (Phyllis Grosskurth, *Melanie Klein. Her World and her Work,* Cambridge, MA: Harvard University Press, 1987, p. 189).

Indeed, whereas normal mourning resembles minimal mania, optimal mourning betokens a zest which is realistic and firm, not idealized and triumphant (Scott, 1964a, pp. 375, 377). It should be emphasized that the repetitive regressions interrupting ego development should be called vicious spirals and not vicious circles, for the repetitions are never the same (Scott, 1985, p. 35).

Of capital theoretical and technical importance is that within the above five overall stages there are three kinds of micro-sequences: impulse-desire-satisfaction; impulse-desire-increasing tension-pain-some disorganization-satisfaction; and impulse-desire-increasing tension-disorganization and hate- regression to sleep. These micro-sequences may be fused, separate, or oscillating in memory, as manifested in dreams and clinical associations. A case in point is depression. In the earliest form of depression, the child becomes aware that he can love and hate the same object that can be both gratifying and frustrating (Scott, 1948a, p. 4). Although appearing together, later manifestations of love and hate might not be fused, but rather oscillate rapidly; if the rapid manifestations can be slowed down to a fraction of a second, the oscillating nature of the ambivalence can be grasped (*Mourning and Zest*, pp. 116-122).

The most distinctive characteristic of Scott's theoretical orientation is his investigation of what I might label the dormancy triangle (going to sleep-sleeping-waking). Broadening his investigation, he has traced the vicissitudes of insomnia, sleepiness, going to sleep, (over)sleep, dreaming (and its relation to hypnosis), waking, and wanting to be awakened, all of which may be remembered, forgotten, or anticipated. As a parallel to what we might call the "ultimate scenes" of conception, birth, and death in our lifespan are the recurrent scenes of the dormancy triangle. We can now understand them as organizing and/or disorganizing scenes in the psychology and psychopathology of everyday life.

Just as Winnicott (1953) speaks of the perpetual task of keeping outer and inner reality of transitional experience separated and yet interrelated, so Scott (1975c, p. 318) wants us to focus on the transitions from being awake to being asleep to being awake. Condensed in these transitions are problems of relationship with the two instincts to the conflict between love and hate. To date, Scott (*ibid.*, p. 263) insists, there has been little in child research about the waking ego's discovery of sleep, its discovery of going to sleep, or its discovery of waking up as well as the integration of going to sleep, sleeping, and awakening. All these discoveries have a continuous history with the widespread difficulties which adults have in sleeping and waking.

Much as Lewin (1964a, p. 374) insisted that all psychopathology must be related to sleep and dream psychology, Scott (1975c) has stressed the clinical neglect of dreaming situation or dormancy triangle in which the dream is

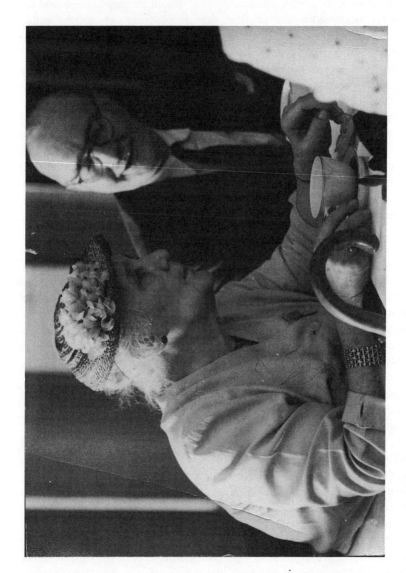

Figure 2. Mrs. M. Klein and Dr. W.C.M. Scott at the IPA Congress in Paris, July-August 1957

set—the activities of waking and sleeping seem all too often relegated to an out-of-bounds reserve or sanctuary, in part because listening to dreams induces sleepiness (ibid., p. 282). Said somewhat differently: there has been an imbalance between the clinical attention accorded to both the analytic process and analytic situation on one hand, and to the dreaming process and the dreaming situation on the other. Scott cautions that the exclusion of the dormancy triangle from analysis is as much a universal amnesia as the infantile amnesia we expect to undo during analysis (ibid., p. 324). Indeed, in his numerous articles and conferences over the years, Scott has not tired of claiming that adequate psychological mindedness must include an a-wakenness to the dormancy triangle. If Freud disturbed sleep of the world, it has somewhat dozed off, and both Lewin and Scott have tried to wake it up again to the richness of dreams and their staging.

The preceding discussion may serve as a contextual setting for the rest of this essay. Since Scott has not written any sustained account of his experience as a child analyst, I have dispersed many of his insights into child psychology throughout my essay's first four parts. The subjects of those four parts are respectively: the dormancy triangle, dreaming, Scott's clinical technique, and his manner of thinking and self-expression. Let it be said that the subjects of the dormancy triangle and dreaming far from exhaust Scott's technique, so that much of what remains to say about it constitutes the fourth part of my essay. I have elected to end with a kind of appendix, a selective collection of Scott's unforgettable clinical vignettes, fittingly entitled "Scotsland."

I. The Dormancy Triangle

a. Going to Sleep

A quick survey of Scott's comments on sleepiness prepares us for his insights into going to sleep itself. The awakened state prior to going to sleep may be analyzed for its defensiveness. When the clinical focus shifts to the defensive history of a patient's sleepiness, working through produces a not only greater perceptiveness and honesty about it but often sleep as well (Scott, 1975c, pp. 276, 342). In this regard, patients report two kinds of blankness, one accompanying sleepiness and the other not, although the latter might be a defense against sleepiness and sleep— oscillations occur-ring between the two blanknesses may come from there being too much content in the inner or the outer world to decide what to talk about (ibid., pp. 295, 297). The blank state described as "I have nothing to talk about" often defends against sleepiness or falling into sleep (Scott, 1952, p. 1); that

Figure 3. Dr. W.C.M. Scott (left), Dr. Hassan Azima and Mrs. Fern Azima (middle) at the 118th Annual Meeting of the American Psychiatric Association, Toronto, May 1962

sleep, let us mind, might itself be a defense rather than a primary state (Scott, 1975c, p. 342). When in fact sleep is defended against by states described as "blankness" and "I have nothing to talk about," Scott's technique is to ask for associations to the question, "If you slept, how would you like to awake or be awakened?" (ibid., p. 314).

The first phase of the dormancy triangle proper is going to sleep. Although Freud spoke of the instinct of sleeping, he neglected to recognize the instincts of going to sleep or waking.[2] If we investigate the instinctual wishes to sleep and the wish to wake in their interrelated totality with all other wishes (ibid., p. 271), we would illuminate the manifestations of narcissism (ibid., p. 342). Heinz Hartmann for his part stressed that we learn about the regressive relationship between the ego and the id by studying falling sleep, a state when the ego abandons itself to the id just as it does in coitus (ibid., p. 323). Rey has suggested that the superego has a different sleep-wake cycle from the ego as regards to the epistemophilic function; perhaps the later conscious superego goes to sleep and the primitive superego with its good and bad objects awakens (Rey, 1992, p. 446).

Regardless of the fact that we all have sleep rituals or ceremonials (Freud, 1915-1917, p. 264), the ability of greater awareness to waking up than to falling sleep (Scott, 1975c, p. 324) has resulted in the relatively few introspective reports on that subject. Going to sleep and waking up may consciously be parts of one and the same short, sudden process and may not be initially separated, as they are later by the consciousness of having slept (ibid., p. 314). A thought of sleep may be a memory or an anticipation of a disguised wish to sleep (ibid., p. 273), but consciousness of breathing is often the last conscious content that we remember (ibid., p. 348).

Going to sleep has its own peculiar history in childhood. It takes time before the child realizes that he cannot say as much about going to sleep as about waking up (ibid., p. 339). The later child's conception of unconscious and conscious is related to his early watching sleepers and remembering himself waking and becoming sleepy and wondering about going to sleep and waking up later (Scott, 1978b). The child changes from initially wanting to sleep with his mother; later, when he goes to sleep, he wants companions in bed partly as a substitute to comfort and to be comforted by—he may put his companions to sleep before he falls asleep, or he may expect them to sleep only after he does and to be there as the first recognizable reality when he wakes (Scott, 1975c, p. 286).

b. Sleep

In that of all the animals, only birds and mammals sleep, human sleep is but a few seconds on the evolutionary scale. Phylogenetically, that is, our

Figure 4. W.C.M. Scott at a New York City meeting (date and occasion unknown)

sleep has a rather recent history. In somewhat parallel theoretical fashion, Freud began by thinking of sleep as an instinct only in the *Outline*, written at the very end of his life. Sleep is a partial instinctive activity in that it recurrently rather than constantly satisfies (Scott, 1975c, pp. 309-310). The object and source of the sleep instinct is the body, and its aim the bodily function leading to satisfaction (Scott, 1986b). That satisfaction is best described by one's state upon waking and the full feeling of having regressed "to the narcissism of oneness, to the world of dreams, with no inner or outer world distinguished" (Scott, 1975c, p. 339).

In the course of our development, sleeping and its normal or abnormal libidinal and aggressive activity in sleeping and waking states, are not well understood (*ibid.*, p. 258). In the absence of the maximal satisfaction in the sequence impulse-satisfaction, a reduced satisfaction in the sequence impulse-desire-tension-pain may result, ending in disorganization, then hate, with a consequent possibility of fatigue and then narcissistic sleep (Scott, 1986b, pp. 7-9). We must recognize two kinds of narcissistic sleep: sleep may be a prime example of the pleasure principle and maximal narcissistic libidinal activity —oceanic bliss; or maximal aggressive narcissistic activity—catastrophic chaos (Scott, 1975a; 1975c, p. 280).

Beliefs, attitudes, and fantasies toward sleep show much variety. In Freud's view, we are aware that we are asleep (Freud, 1900, p. 571); he himself felt a "somnambulistic certainty" that he placed a long lost and forgotten object in a desk drawer which he then opened (Freud, 1901, p. 140). Other evidence of the activity which goes on even in sleep is the exceptional time sense that only some people have in sleep (Scott, 1975c, p. 331). Duration of sleep-need perhaps varies more from person to person than any other primary need except perhaps orgasmic need (*ibid.*, p. 348). The two-year-old child not only shows increased difficulty in going to sleep, but he has difficulty in getting out of sleep; he temporarily loses the knack of waking up, but at adolescence he may show a similar clinging to sleep (Scott, 1948b, p. 145). A child can also get annoyed at not being able to stay awake to find out what it is like to be asleep (Scott, 1976b).[3] Generally speaking, fantasies about sleep can range from hallucination about being asleep (Scott, 1975c, p. 278), to the commoner introjections or projections, namely, "Do I go into something or does something go into me?", "Do I go into sleep or am I overcome by sleep?", "Does it go into me?" (*ibid.*, p. 311). Finally, in times of danger, such as war, those who sleep best were often those who had come to terms with the possibilities of being killed while awake or asleep (*ibid.*, p. 259), and they awoke with a short-lived cathexis of an omnipotent creative wish and its fulfillment, i.e., "a world and an ego are created" (*ibid.*, p. 279).

Scott's technical reflections about sleep are worthy of note. First of all,

Figure 5. Dr. W.C.M. Scott (left) with Drs. Elie Debanne (middle) and Austin Lee (right) (1994)

sleeping with a person or being with a person who sleeps is rarely mentioned in analysis, perhaps on account of both transference and counter-transference problems (*ibid.*, p. 347). Analytic treatment, we should acknowledge, may progress "when equal importance is given to the interpretation of repression of concern about sleep, and the frustration of having to wake up to tell dreams" (*ibid.*, p. 327). What is more, we must analyze the patient's early childhood stages of real anger and pleasure, frustration and satisfaction in relation to the issue of sleep during sessions (*ibid.*, p. 318).

If more attention is paid to defenses against sleeping and looking as well as to their substitute and primary instinctive aspects, an increased amount of sleeping and looking may enter the analytic situation (Scott, 1952, p. 5). Scott found that with patients resisting sleep, the easiest way to bring the nature of the aim of the sleep wish into consciousness was to ask for associations to the question, "If you slept, how would you like to wake or be wakened?" (*ibid.*, p. 1). But if they seem to sleep, his technique was to ask them whether or not they were sleeping at least five minutes before the end of the interview (Scott, 1975c, p. 295). The analyst should bear in mind that talking with patients about consciousness and unconsciousness and partial instincts related to sleep often leads to defensive silence or verbal confusion, a confusion comparable to the trouble a child has in talking about sleep and in going to sleep (*ibid.*, p. 338).

c. Waking

Although we ignore what waking before birth is like, we do know that the source of the waking instinct is the body; its aim, the bodily function leading to satisfaction; and its object, the body from its surface to its depths (Scott, 1986b). The origin of the waking instinct dates back to the uterine conflict between sleeping and waking (*ibid.*). Our life began by waking, not sleeping; thus, the core psychic unit in our lives is waking-sleeping and not the contrary (Scott, 1975c, p. 278). The instinct of sleeping fuses with waking from the dream state and fuses again with the later waking state when the dream is remembered (Scott, 1987b). But it is an open question as to when sleepiness and wakefulness are first connected with sleep (Scott, 1975a, p. 350).

Being instinctually motivated, the wishes to sleep and to wake are rooted in the unconscious (*ibid.*, p. 268). Consciousness is an instinct, whose first object is the dawn of ego-object relations in its minimal or narcissistic form (*ibid.*, p. 338). At the point of waking, the conflicts between the wish to sleep, the wish to wake, the wish to dream, the wish to remember the dream and the wish to forget the dream may be condensed (Scott, 1975a). Those conflicts, ranging from transitory to persistent, affect the breadth and intensity of our awakenness (Scott, 1990a). Perhaps the first defense on waking is against unconscious processes which would lead to a wake-dream or hallucinosis (Scott, 1975c, p. 277).

Mothers teach children to go to sleep, but they wake up in their own way (Scott, 1986b). Although we slowly learn that we did not create the world to which we wake (Scott, 1990b), the change from the state before sleep to waking may at times be felt as sudden or even magically omnipotent (Scott, 1975c, p. 339). A world and an ego are born (Scott, 1952, p. 1)! Not only can waking up be slowed down, but it can also be speeded to become as fast as anything we can do, thus it might act as a defense against being conscious of the transition from sleep to waking, or from dream to memory of dream, or to perception (Scott, 1975c, p. 280). Adult experiences of greatest speeds and sudden change can often by reconstructed by going back to the infantile discovery of the slowness or speed of going to sleep and waking up. The child is apt to have the illusion of his sleeping and waking as simultaneous, and only later, by realizing that it has slept for some time, understand the "sudden change" and the difference of the two activities (*ibid.*, p. 343).

A big problem is a lack of concern about that which happens in dreams, if anything, before we wake up, and which can become a dream residue upon our waking. This waking up to something we were never awake to before is very related to creativeness which may loosen primary repression as distinguished from secondary repression (Scott, 1986b).[4] In his last paper of 1979, Bion wrote of wake work on the remembered dream while we are awake (Scott, 1986b). It was the early Freud, however, who coined and thrice used the term "wakework."[5] Just as we carry out dream work on the dream in sleep, we do wake work on the remembered dream while we are awake (Scott, 1990a).[6]

We know much about the later derivatives of looking and sleeping (e.g. the visual sleep dream) but little about the origins of the connection between looking and waking (Scott, 1952, p. 3; 1975c, p. 260). Since optical fixation is a physical voluntary innervation possible in the awakened stage only, a person in a dream eagerly trying to read something will wake imminently (Scott, 1975c, p. 260).[7] Prominent examples of infantile wancies are the following: Will the baby find mother inside on waking? Will baby wake to being inside mother, and for a time believe all he sees and hears, is mother's insides? Will the world into which baby wakes be a world without mother, without a meal, and only cries and perhaps a sad repeated journey of troubles, until all ends well again as part of repeating but changing cycles? (Scott, 1990b). More complex wancies include Lewin's well-known triad of oral wishes (to eat, be eaten, and sleep). That triad may also appear in passive-active terms (to feed, sleep, to eat into, versus to be fed, to be put to sleep, to be eaten). Projective-introjective dynamics underlie other wishful variants (to be fed, to be eaten, to be encompassed by sleep versus to feed, to eat into, to encompass sleep) (Scott, 1975c, p. 341).

There are many stages of sleepiness discovered during the development of different ways of waking. We can wake up to forgetting, or forgetting that we have forgotten, or remembering to remember (Scott, 1986b).[8] Sooner or later one wakes to remember that he awoke; one wakes to being awake to being awake and begins to anticipate sleeping (Scott, 1987b). Proclaiming his advanced thinking in those papers delivered in 1986 and 1987, Scott tried to heal the broken links between the polar instincts of sleep, unawareness and the unconscious on the one hand, and waking, awareness, and consciousness on the other. He questioned whether we add anything to the term "waking" by saying that we are "aware" or "conscious"—whether, that is, we are merely giving a new name to the meaning of reflection. Although it would be quite a linguistic exercise to describe to a child what "aware of being awake" means (Scott, 1986b), we can talk to our colleagues about awareness and consciousness as well as unawareness and unconsciousness. Would it not be clearer, Scott proposes, to say "awake to being awake," thus being explicit about the type of reflection? (Scott, 1990a).[9]

The transitional states of going to sleep and waking up are rarely talked about after infancy, even in treatment (Scott, 1987b). The need to understand the types of conflict and the speed and manner with which they are solved may be a long time coming into any analysis. In the treatment of these issues, so many repetitions of early types of waking, alone or with someone who was awake or asleep, have to be worked through (Scott, 1975a).

Ever pursuing insight into the dynamics of sleeping, waking and sleep-wake conflicts, Scott interpreted defenses against the indifference to memories of sleep and awaking (Scott, 1990a). Yet he readily admitted the difficulty in deciding how awake or asleep patients are, or how fused, confused, or quickly oscillating are their states of sleeping and waking (Scott, 1987a). During interviews, moreover, some examples of fast waking and some examples of fast falling asleep were used as defenses against memories of a sleep dream or a day dream. Scott urged the reconstruction of the defenses against waking up for the 3-4 a.m. feeding and the reactions to the first regularly missed feeding and other experiences of waking up and not being fed, which led to memories of waiting (Scott, 1952, p. 2; 1975c, p. 342).

Patients may also keep themselves awake for fear that they would sleep too long (Scott, 1975c, p. 346). When someone remains unconscious of having awakened, he or she may come to the interview and, instead of telling a dream, will talk as if the analytic situation is continuing a dream. To change that situation, we must interpret the patient's denial of having awakened, or interpret their delusion of still being asleep and being able to wake up in the place where they went to sleep (*ibid.*, p. 325).

It is also instructive to follow Scott's technique with patients having serious waking problems. Two of his clinical examples merit citation:

> Twice I have interpreted that a certain female patient was waking in her sleep, that she believed me to be part of a dream in which, if she woke, she would be in bed at home, but I believed that she woke. In both instances, the patient suddenly changed; she was confused in finding herself awake in session and remembered dreaming of being in analysis with me, then went to sleep again and came to the interview the next day walking in her sleep (Scott, 1987a, p. 13).

> A manic depressive who would not lie down during the first months of treatment took sedation for sleeplessness. She would fall into stupors from which, as she said, she suddenly woke up. My interpretations of anxieties about going to sleep were ineffective until I addressed her anxieties about waking up. Then it became apparent that sleep was death for her and that she felt that my interpretations were fostering her suicide. Later she spoke of perplexity as to whether she was awake or not, and on one occasion after this she asked me not to awaken her lest the awful things come to be. I interpreted this as a delusion of sleep—that she was treating me as her dream, as an entirely internal object (Scott, 1975c, p. 296).

II. Dreaming

Scott devoted major attention to dreaming, the activity that is literally embedded within the dormancy triangle. The instincts of sleeping and waking are fused and can be conflicted in dreaming (Scott, 1990a).[10] Our sleep restores primitive narcissism and effects the withdrawal of cathexes of consciousness until broken through by the consciousness of the dream; with sleep as its preconscious part, the dream itself recapitulates the history of disillusionment of primary narcissism, which, to an important extent, occurs upon one's waking from earlier dreams (Scott, 1975c, pp. 256, 284, 308).[11] Some children and adults can tolerate and exploit fantasy which is near to hallucinosis in vividness; in others, the ego's contribution to the sleep-dream may also be the wish to dream rather than to hallucinate (*ibid.*, p. 277)—a dynamic supporting Garma's insistence that the fulfillment of a wish is a dream's defense against the primary revival of the trauma in hallucinated form (*ibid.*, p. 282). Scott also investigated sleep and dreams that are themselves hallucinated instead of being remembered (*ibid.*, p. 259).

In the case of many unremembered dreams, the waking ego is envious of the dream function and spoils the link between the dream and waking life (Scott, 1974).

Scott's insatiable interest in dreams has extended to every type: those of the feeble-minded (Scott, 1975a); the dream with laughter in it (*ibid*); the vaguest or minimal dream—Lewin's dream screen or blank dream (Scott, 1975c, p. 313); the hateful oneiric kind ending in the satisfaction of hate, and the convulsive and traumatic, hateful kind leading to pain (Scott, 1953a); and the most difficult dreams in which a person sleeps and wakes up in the dream (Hunter, 1995, p. 203). Scott has noted dreams themselves rarely contain sleeping people or timepieces and rarely about the dream state (Scott, 1975c, p. 324). And he has found that the dualistic-laden images of the mirror and horizon frequently symbolize sleeping and waking (*ibid*., pp. 342-343). According to his further findings, premenstrual dreams are apt to be erotic, and postmenstrual ones maternal (*ibid*., p. 254). And he has identified the type "vista dreams," which, arriving at a critical change in the analysis, span much of the patient's life and require an interpretive attention lasting over many sessions (Scott, 1974; 1975c, p. 263).[12] Scott (1990a) regrets that he had neither a patient who dreamt of being hypnotized nor one who, if he slept, associated to hypnosis.

Reports of children's dreams have a special place in Scott's writing. It happens in a child's dream that he goes into mother, or that his very dream remains outside or even disappears deep inside. In one instance, "the dream vanished into a cupboard in the room, the door of which was too heavy and the catch too complicated for the child to manipulate, and he did not wish to tell the secret to any adult whom he might have asked to help him—the place represented the interior of his mother's body" (Scott, 1975c, pp. 316, 344). Scott has observed that the child may dream about his attempts to understand the beginning of speech and so dream of spoken speech and understood and then upon waking, hear mother's voice and is only able to baby-talk (*ibid*., p. 344). He has suggestively asked whether the infant who wakes and babbles to itself and returns to sleep is babbling about babbling or about waking, dreaming, and sleeping (*ibid*., p. 282). He has urged analysts to learn a notation to register the sound a patient heard in a dream, which itself was a memory of an earlier sound, e.g., a memory of an attempt to imitate mother's sound or a memory of an attempt to get mother to imitate its sound (private communication, 1976).

According to Scott's observations, the child's development of boundaries prepares him both to understand and tolerate the phenomenon of the double in his dreaming and nondreaming life. But for the double to have meaning, the child must first solve some of his problems with internalization and externalization, as well as with the stabilization of the inside-out and outside-in. The child, that is to say, must first be able to incorporate the world on going to sleep and externalize it upon waking, and he must develop stable boundaries that lead to feelings of outsideness, insideness, and besideness (Scott, 1975c, p. 342). If, however, the child's dreams are exciting, or frightening, he may still be confused about the person waking him up and about what he remembers (or hallucinates) of the not yet forgotten or not yet disappeared dream. This situation is especially confusing when the dream contains the persons who have come to wake the young sleeper—or then again, the child may be desirously dreaming of his mother, only to be woken by his father (Scott, 1986c). An enlightening contrast is found in the example of the psychotic who, upon waking, had a hallucinatory regression to the time before he could discriminate and tolerate his dream as a double of the external world (Scott, 1975c, p. 340).

The I-thou experience has its roots in the discovery of the double: "I the hallucinator-rememberer-anticipator/thou the hallucination-memory-anticipation" versus "I the perceiver/thou the perception." Repetitions of this discovery sometimes occur when a patient in session, instead of first bringing up his awakening perceptions and their relation to the dream, talks immediately about the dream from which he has just awakened (Scott, 1976b). A complication arises when the analyst figures in such a dream; if the patient sleeps in order to deny the analyst's doubleness and thus to make him only into an internal figure, he must eventually wake and overcome this frustration by talking (Scott, 1975c, p. 349). We come upon a further complication when a dreamy patient suddenly realizes that he has not recognized that he was talking to himself rather than to the analyst; one reason for this is that the patient may remember playing the peek-a-boo game with his mother—the game of talking and looking away and looking back, the game of magical appearance and disappearance, magical destruction and recreation, and maintaining a memory and then discovering the double of the memory in the external world (ibid., pp. 341-342).

Scott's technique with dreams also shows his originality. In an overall sense, he has extended Ferenczi's comparison of the analytic session to a dream: its beginning can be symbolic of going to sleep, its ending symbolic of waking,[13] with the analyst figuring in that pervasive dream (ibid., p. 349). Scott went on to consider that repression is the most important aspect of patients' dreams in the analytic situation (ibid., p. 327), an idea foreshadowed in Freud's (1925, p. 128) tenet that dreams best fill their function if they are forgotten (in the words of Lewin [1975c], "to remember the dream is a quasi prolongation of sleep... while forgetting the dream repeats and stands for waking up" [Scott, ibid., p. 323]).[14] To that effect, Scott (1986b) is ever alert to interpret the part played by both the ego and superego in forgetting. Believing that certain things could be discovered only if they sleep and dream in session, some patients fend off sleep and even repress the wish to sleep in the presence of the analyst (ibid., p. 346); they may even engage in talk as a defense of dreaming about being in/away from analysis or as a defense to wish for a dreamless or a more talkful sleep (ibid., p. 277).

Throughout Scott's clinical work the relationship of minor disorders of both sleeping and waking to the forgetting and remembering of dreams[15] is at the forefront (ibid., p. 256). He also keeps in view the optimal relationship among specific acts of dreams, sleep, and waking (ibid., p. 284). Equally important are the connections between the manifest dream and the patient's first thought on waking, his manner of waking, and his emergent attitudes to the dream (ibid., p. 332). Scott has found that in the fear that their dreams will bore the analysts, some patients identify with aggressive parents who once rejected or forgot their child's dreams. The child who called out on waking up might have been told, "Go back to sleep," or "You've only been dreaming"; and the next morning he might not have been asked to remember the dream and talk about it (ibid., pp. 36, 327-328).[16]

Scott has specified a number of ways in which he has extended the concept of day residue. For example, there is both dream residue and wake residue in the next day's dream. A depressive dream may continue as a residue fended off by a manic, wakeful state (Scott, 1964a, p. 374). When a patient dreams on the couch, the day residues can include a sessional immediacy.[17] In the remembered dream, in the background there is always the dreamer's wish that in the next sleep he will continue the dream in the next sleep. Such a continued dream will involve as day residue, the dreamer's memory of being awake the day before and of what he did with the dream (Scott, 1975c, p. 288).

If for Freud dreams are the royal road to the unconscious, for Scott dreams during the analytic session are the shortest royal road to the unconscious and to infantile amnesia.[18] To those patients who cannot remember their dream, Scott interprets their possible regret upon waking that he was not present there when the dream might have been remembered and told immediately (ibid., p. 324). When he thought the sleeping patient was dreaming, he would wake him and ask to be told the dream right away, the point being that the account might differ from one given by the dreamer who would wake up of his own accord (Scott, 1964b).[19] But in Scott's general understanding, the reported dream may be taken as the first association to the dream itself (Scott, 1975c, p. 332).[20]

Mindful of Freud's observation that our thought activity changes to images as sleep takes over, Scott was interested in the issues of visuality and light in dreams. Two of his vignettes about technical management may suffice. In one patient, the feeling that everything was brighter when she closed her eyes was related to her idealized wake-dreams that ever since childhood contained light brighter than day. While working through the link between wake-dreams and sleep-dreams, their light began to show variations similar to the variations of the light. Another patient once slept and woke up without opening his eyes and wondered whether the light he saw was a memory of the light of the dream or the light of a lamp in the room coming through his eyelids. Scott discovered that the light represented the external analyst, whereas the internal light represented his dream, himself, and what he had already obtained from others. The patient opened his eyes to discover the room darker than expected, a circumstance reflecting his belief that he had obtained more from Scott in the past than he expected to obtain in the shorter time left in the analysis (*ibid.*, pp. 342-343).[21]

III. Scott's Clinical Technique

A few introductory words should be said about Scott's organization of the analytic setting and framework. He places a rather wide couch away from the wall, thus putting the patient in a freer space that facilitates his free association. Reflecting his stress on the patient's body schema and regression to early stages, Scott had a cloth at hand since he felt Kleenex was inadequate for "a bout of really active crying"; he also had a blanket available, as well as a bowl ready for vomiting (Scott, 1970). Drawing on his own experience of having two analytic sessions a day for a certain period, Scott (1984b) holds that every analytical candidate should have longer sessions for a period in his personal analysis and should also offer them to his own patients (*ibid.*, p. 150).

A key Heisenberg principle guiding Scott's technique concerns the necessity that we be aware of our procedural limitations from the very onset of any analysis. The more we are supposedly "objective" and refrain from altering the observational scene, the less we interpret and the less we learn about a patient's ability to change; but the more we interpret, the more we disturb our perceptions about the patient's mental status at rest (Scott, 1964b, p. 4; 1962, p. 346.). In a private communication (1976), Scott showed further how Heisenberg's principle of indeterminacy undercuts clinical observation:

> The mouth may speak what the body part spoken of cannot speak, and in fact, a child may say that he is saying what the part would say if it could speak. The difficulty of speaking about speech and speaking about the mouth is also relevant insofar as the very act of speaking changes the sensation in the mouth from the sensation which was intended to be spoken about. A memory rather than an ongoing sensation has to be spoken about.

Such phenomena are necessarily altered as one tries to explain them to different audiences, such as to the child patient, to his mother, and to one's colleagues with different training and competence (*Becoming an Analyst*, pp. 108-112; Rey, 1992, p. 3).

Driven by his own curiosity and sympathetic understanding (1981b, p. 4), Scott incited his patient to be ever more truthfully curious (*Becoming an Analyst*, p. 11). To this end, Scott (1986c) interpreted in order that the patient became free to associate in questions, much like the child saying: "What's that? What's that? What's that?" (*ibid.*, p. 9). To stimulate his own curiosity, Scott (1982b) kept in mind Henry Rey's (1992) interrogatory formula: "What part of the subject, when and where, in what state and for what intention, does what, to what part of the object, when and where, and with what consequences for both the subject and the object?" (p. 56). Concomitant with those self-reminders is Scott's (1985) particular focus on the corporeal schema as perceived consciously or symbolically by the patient. A turning point in Scott's technique occurred when he began to ask patients to try to tell everything that they *could* say, rather than everything that came to their mind (Scott, 1985)—but the problem remains of their proneness to indulge in recounting the past instead of the present, and to narrate what happened instead of what is happening (Scott, 1975b).

Lastingly impressed by Adolf Meyer's tenet that "whatever makes a difference is significant" (*Mourning and Zest*, p. 189), Scott (1984a) strove to have his patients join him in being "wakefully discriminatory" (*ibid.*, p. 462). Included in that observational goal are the speed, length, sequencing and repetitions of events—the repetitions themselves are important for containing inevitable significant differences and for possibly indicating a defensiveness toward new behavior (*Mourning and Zest*, p. 197). Scott (1984b) also noted how patients made their maximal discriminations and greatest integrations of what they were part of and what their words were for "everything that exists" (*ibid.*, p. 152). Affective and temporal factors, however, interfere with the capacity to discriminate. Thus, when aggression and anxiety are maximal, there is hardly a chance of making discriminating perceptions and accepting symbolizing activity (*ibid.*, p. 153). Temporally, an accelerated oscillation may lead to confusion and even elude perceptual discrimination (Scott, 1986c). Since the period of oscillation must be reduced to the region of 1/10 to 1/100 second before the elements are consciously discriminated and seen as discontinuous, the patient's awareness of ambivalence and its components will be accordingly affected (1953b). From the analyst's point of view, first the patient's inactivity will be detectable, then confusion, and finally the oscillation between recognizable love and hate (*ibid.*).

It is quite revelatory of Scott's (1962) corporeal orientation in assessing pathology that to Anna Freud's list of factors (such as frustration tolerance, anxiety tolerance and capacity for substitution) he added the rate of growth and sleep patterns, and variations of orgasm, fertility, parturition, and lactation as well as speed of reaction (*ibid.*, p. 239). Given the variations in sensorial sensitivity, Scott urged that we observe the greatest and least importance that patients individually lend to touching and being touched, tasting and being tasted, smelling and being smelled, hearing and being heard, and seeing and being seen (private communication). It was only gradually, however, that Scott thought of certain similarities between child and adult analysis that extended to both ego development and emergence of new discriminations and visual fields between analyst and analysand, all being related to the child's early nondiscrimination between a mouthful and an eyeful (Scott, 1970).[22]

Scott (1984a) has recurrently insisted on the analyst's discrimination that is crucial to decide whether transference is a regressive or a progressive defense rather than more related to insightfully working through (*ibid.*, p. 463). Hopelessness or minimal hopefulness may give rise to pathological regressions and pathological progressions (*Mourning and Zest*, p. 168). The always present possibility of regression to magical restitution and progression to reparation are often confused both in patients and in clinical descriptions, the clarification of that confusion being indispensable for analytic progress (private communication). To that effect Scott (1986a) helped patients work through sado-masochistic developments, manic denial, and idealization so that they would become zestful in reparative resolution. Especially in transitional depressive-manic periods (Scott, 1960, p. 500), Scott closely watched sequences of behavior, the slow or sudden changes of emotions, and their pinpoint balances, with the aim of assisting patients to go from a confusional state of tolerating oscillating affects to the satisfied state of tolerating their complexity (*ibid.*, p. 502).

A principle element in Scott's (1986b) technical armamentarium was his particular way to foster the remembering of broken links and forging of new ones in every session. Scott attempted to link: (1) preparing to sleep, dream, and wake; (2) the subsequent sleeping and dreaming; and (3) the waking to remember some dreaming and going on to daydream about the dream and eventually beginning to plan to act. "Why," Scott advanced, "can't we talk about the links between everything, something, and nothing? Why can't we talk more easily about all times, sometimes, and never?" (Scott, 1990a). Scott (1986c) also wanted to be the person "who speaks to the young child, or to the child in the adult, using words to make a link with the early experience of the nothing prior to its anger-motivated transformation into something" (p. 16). In that fashion, Scott underlined the child's angry, transitional intolerance of nothing and held out as exemplary Bion's attention to less and less, enabling him to discover how a symbol of nothing could become the beginning of thinking.

Tapping on his own infantile anxiety about becoming too spontaneously loving and happy (*Becoming a Psychoanalyst*, p. 162), Scott often interpreted that patients fear "becoming too spontaneously loving and happy like a baby and remembering the early years when they were too spontaneous, too loving—so that somebody stopped them" (Hunter, 1995, p. 196). In a further development of interpretive technique, Scott (1981a) asked patients about their memories and anticipatory fantasies of maximal experiences,[23] e.g., when they were happiest, angriest, saddest, most frightened, most guilty, most fatigued, and in the greatest pain, as well as under what circumstances could they imagine becoming so in the future.

Visual activity plays a cardinal role in Scott's (1970) analytic treatment. A basic premise grounding his practice is that despite fixated impressions, our looking is actually a continuous scanning, since the two to ten saccadic eye movements per second escape our conscious awareness. In his observation of infants, he concluded that sometimes they gape or have an open mouth or eyes, as if they are discovering a nothing, an absence, or the disappearance of hallucination (private communication). Looking can become more remarkably complicated in actual child analysis: the child frequently talks about wanting the therapist to watch; or wanting the therapist to watch him watch the therapist do something; or even wanting to watch the therapist do something without being able to watch him watch the therapist.

Scott has made an additional number of fascinating interpretations about the impact of fantasy on visual perception in adult analysis. The patient who feels that he is being stared at rarely mentions that it is with one eye or the other—actually, one has to be some distance away from anyone to become conscious of the fact that one can look at both eyes, rather than at one or the other. Although it is not possible to judge correctly whether one is being looked at mostly on the chin, right eye or left eye, people mostly have the illusion that they can tell. Some patients may persevere by looking at the analyst and hoped that his expression will change, thus a defense against looking away or closing the eyes to see more clearly what the wish is. Looking at a minor detail of facial expression will often stimulate the wish or act to fend off the wish to analyze the analyst. Mutually concurrent talking by the analyst and patient is less compatible than a mutually concurrent looking, which is often related to kissing, fighting and other mutual acts.

Scott (1970) also has found that patients repeat habits they formed in childhood when they were trying to discover many aspects of their body, especially when they were curious about how much they gave out and took in with their eyes and mouth. Such patients may show inhibited partial stretching, yawning, and other significant body movements. Other patients may be looking through or into the analyst, putting him into the distance, bringing him close, or bringing inside only as an image (Scott, 1976a).

Scott does not hesitate to alter the visuality of the analytic setting. For the purpose of fostering development after the transference has been understood, he might have the patient speak to him before a mirror and relate his attendant inhibitions in so doing. In those difficult periods where another analyst might invite the patient to sit up, Scott (1985) preferred to see whether his sitting at the foot of the couch would put the patient at ease. Also, when patients brought in memories of the way they looked and talked or wanted to do so, he often moved a chair toward the foot of the couch near the patient's feet. Scott (1970) explained, "If a patient is facing me but can very easily look away, I can observe his expression when he looks at me or elsewhere, and I then detect the relationship between speech, memory, anticipation and looking" (p. 11).

Two relevant vignettes further demonstrate Scott's clinical flexibility and inventiveness:

1. Once while treating a depressed patient who at times became stuporous and stared straight ahead, I interpreted how the content of the visual field became a substitute easing her to wait for what was wanted in the mouth. During my interpretation, I began to walk around the couch into the patient's visual field so that my speech and her sight of me were part of the same experience. My previous interpretations in an unaltered setting had not been so effective (Scott, 1970, p. 18).

2. On another occasion, Scott (1985) relied on a different visual parameter. I asked a patient to try self-analyzing before a mirror for three minutes in my consultation room because she wanted to work alone. Upon my return to the room, she said that she had been incapable of speaking and looking at the mirror. When I placed my chair between the mirror and her, she discovered that I did not change as much as she had expected and then became capable of perceiving for an instant the excitement on her own face (p. 44).

Scott's technical handling of the analytic setting also attended to its many acoustic aspects, including the inhibition, repression, and transformation of noise. Sometimes he explained the counsel of free association to patients this way: Try to talk, and if you can't talk, try to make some kind of noise, and if you don't know what kind of noise to make, just guess. By inviting the patient to lie down, Scott affirmed, it is as if we are asking him to regress to the period when the baby cannot sit but can roll around and make plenty of noise (Scott, 1975b)—the period of the child's native tongue preceding the acquisition of his mother tongue (Scott, 1989). Scott's (1958) working hypothesis was that when speech is used as a defense against noise, analysis may be slowed; however, when patients understand that noise just as well as speech may speed and foster analysis, they will make more noise (p. 1).[24] On such occasions Scott (1952) may have also imitated the non-verbal sound the patient made (p. 4).

Scott's understanding of the repertoire of noises is instructive. Screams of sobs and joy lead to fatigue; screams of rage can last much longer (private communication). Significant clapping in body movement may extend to inhibited hand-clapping and knee-clapping, etc. (Scott, 1958, p. 4). The ambiguous sound "ah," meaning no, yes, or a question, may be reversed into "ha" or combined into "aha", "ugh,"which is often taken as a sound of disgust, may be a sound of welcome bringing the internal and the external object together, or it may represent "a return of the swallow," as one patient put it (Scott, 1958, p. 2).

Elaborating on noises, Scott (1958) wondered why analysts had not become more clinically interested in the problems of those who had to learn to speak in belch after having lost by operation part or all of their larynx (p. 2). Persistent snores may obtain gratification combined with denial of the noise of the sleep-disrupting snore.[25] Sniffing may show disdain but also unconscious or conscious agreement. A short snort is usually related to the rejection or ejection of something unpleasant or to inhibited laughter (attempts to put the snort into words usually produce laughter). Between the upper noises of the larynx (such as belches) and the lower noises of bowel and bladder lie borborygmi; these are liable to occur at significant moments as derivatives of swallowing-belching, or anal output. A defensive interrelation may exist among alternate coughing, burping, and bopping. Finally, an inhibition of speech may sometimes be due to the oscillation of noises inside: a certain patient felt that no matter what kind of noise she might make, a nice noise would have to be followed by a nasty one, and vice versa (ibid., p. 3).

Scott brought to the fore other locutory variations in the analytic scene. He stated that sometimes a patient, while keeping his mouth wide open but not listening, may watch the movements of the analyst's lips and tongue. Such cathexis equally shared by open eyes and mouth gives the opportunity of interpreting regression to the time of lack of discrimination between the eyes and noise made by the mother and the rest of the world (Scott, 1952, p. 4). Analysts also confront the problem of who is listening: Is the patient listening to what he says? Does he make his audience his only listener? (Scott, 1975b). Is there an inner analyst being spoken to when a patient's voice drops or when a patient remarks that he has forgotten where is or was (Scott, 1976a)?

Scott reflected on still other possibilities:

> Sometimes I would be able to say something simple and noticed that the patient did not stop talking though his or her face registered a reaction to what I said. Sometimes I noticed that when I said something, a patient might begin to speak, but when I was silent, he or she fell silent as well (*Becoming a Psychoanalyst*, pp. 195-196).

In the final account, analysts will agree with Scott (1976a) that, except some singers and actors, few patients in analysis overcome their inhibitions to put anger, joy, or sadness into anything like the energetic speech approximating the energy of their primary noise. Taking one more step, Scott (1981b) proposed that self-analysis be carried out not by closing one's self up in inner speech but rather by talking to one's self out loud—such an analysand's zest for self-analysis relates to his belief about the good role he played in the self-analysis of his own analyst.

IV. Scott's Manner of Thinking and Self-Expression

Scott had a remarkable ability to empathize with and convey the infant's mental world. Closely bound up with mode of infantile perception and expression but not identical with it are the condensing and displacing characteristics of primary process, all of which Scott could subject to acute analysis. When at its best, his mentational and scriptive manner illuminated and mimetically dramatized its message—and in such moments one can detect a definite change in the tone of Scott's prose with its quickened rhythms. At other times, the balance was tipped, so that a removed, analytic perspective was lost, and the pace of rational elaboration gives way to expository confusion marked by impulsive thrusts of fantasy-like associativeness—or to mix metaphors, at other times in his discourse Scott seemlessly sewed his own comments into a child's phantasmagoria and interior monologue. The upshot is that the reader was offered streams of marvelous insights swirling into each other.

To further delineate Scott's communicative style, I find Einstein's timely yet troubling counsel to scientific writers most serviceable: "we write either correctly or understandably." Seen within the context of Einstein's maxim, Scott, although striving for accuracy, tried to say so much or even too much at once. Expository control was not his forte. Although he had made several attempts to organize the grander design of psychoanalytic thought, he

struggled to maintain a controlled logical progression over sustained pieces of writing. It is often easy to shuffle his paragraphs and longer expository units like a deck of cards, without any resultant difference in thematic development. Even within Scott's paragraphs and individual sentences, one tends to miss a tight logical coherence—his efforts at linking are undercut by awkward punctuation and syntax (incidentally, the latter word from an etymological point of view means placing together or linking).

A related problem inhabits Scott's aim of communicative simplicity. On one hand, he wanted "to lead a simpler life by using simpler words and playing the game of small words in long sentences and long stories" (Scott, 1986b, p. 1). On the other hand, that aim was subverted by his endorsement of Whorf's postulate that the more a word is used the shorter it becomes and the more meanings it has (Scott, 1986c), a phenomenon that also affected the language of science (*Mourning and Zest*, pp. 28-29). In effect, Scott (1986c) resembled both Freud and Bion, who, he said, were more multiguous than ambiguous. Yet within that multiguity or in spite of it, Scott (1970) bemoaned the fact that our current technical terms, although adequately describing later stages of development, did not suffice for the earlier elemental stage. "We need to do so much work," Scott (1987a) reminded us, "to put into words what happened before words were understood or used" (*ibid.*, p. 8).

In reading and listening to Scott over a number of years, I have been ever impressed by the paradoxical freshness and lawful patterning of his creative discourse. While analyzing it, I have drawn up a series of ad hoc categories (they also may be used, however, as an analytical grid in the mapping out of infantile mentation and adult phantasy life). Within each of the thirteen categories I have furnished clarifying examples drawn from Scott's texts:

1. *Klang association*:
   a. "Analysis works to undo the ignorance summed up in the maxim 'I wit, I wot but I forgot' or 'I understand that I understood but I've forgotten'" (private communication).
   b. "I wit, I wot, but I forgot. Mind is such an odd predicament for matter to get into. What is matter? Never mind. What is mind? Never matter" (Scott, 1975c, p. 1).

2. *Thingification of thought*:
   a. "But soon there's a difference between 'I've forgotten' and 'I remember.' I don't know where the forgotten is. Is the forgotten inside or outside? Is it in me or in them?" (Hunter, 1995, p. 97).
   b. "If delusion went away, what was it replaced by? When did it (pain, etc.) come from? When did it go? Into whom?" (private

communication).

3. *The maximal and the minimal*:

   a. "In order to find out the smallest sound that they can hear, children listen closely to the soap bubble as they prick it or they click their nails with less and less force" (private communication).

   b. "We go about trying to make an even better best of a sadder job" (private communication).

   c. "How does one establish the difference and continuity between minimal linkage and maximal splitting?" (Scott, 1984b, p. 154).

   d. "We must study the greatest and least changes happening within both the longest and shortest periods of time, and when does oscillation become confusion" (private communication, 1994).

4. *The play of opposites*:

   In conversation with Jones, Freud said that when he felt stymied in thinking out a problem, he recalled the counsel of his own private maxim: "Think of the opposite." On pages 185-186 of his autobiography Scott reported that piece of conversational exchange correctly; but elsewhere, a distortion in Scott's cryptomnesic account sheds insight into his own thought processes. Hence we read that Freud counseled thinking about as many opposites as possible when in difficulty (Scott, 1986c). In so giving the screw another turn, Scott (1987a) maximizes the opposite into the greatest number of opposites, a maximalization which he joins with klang association in another essay: "the problem is, which opposite is the most apposite?" (p. 4). In a still further turn of the screw, he sought uncommonly thought of opposites in asking about the opposite of experience and of intuition (*Becoming a Psychoanalyst*, pp. 185-186).

5. *Spatial distortion and discrimination*:

   a. "When babies are frustrated, they try to get inside flatness, for example, a flat piece of paper. Then they can crumble up the paper and then get inside it" (private communication).

   b. "How does the child know the difference between inside out and outside in? A certain child said: 'I was in the dream, but the dream is gone, and I am where am I now'" (private communication).

   c. "The feeling that all is inside and nothing outside and one of its opposites—all is outside and nothing inside—are descriptions of maximal introjective and projective identification" (Scott, 1975c, p. 315).

   d. "We grow to realize the difference between our backside and a world behind in contrast to learning about the difference between the world in front and our front-side. We did this all, helped by many sleeps and dreams, and by many wakings to use our senses to sort out insides, besides, and outsides and to sort out facts and fancies" (Scott, 1990b, p. 6).

6. *Spatio-temporal distortions*:
    a. "We come to believe in growth and try to watch our hair and nails grow, but only believe our whole body has grown when we remember how much smaller it was then than now. The penis or clitoris may change in size and feeling and this may be confused with growth, as the child can wake to, or be awakened to the speed at which tumescence happens" (Scott, 1987a, p. 10).
    b. "Another question is: Can I go everywhere? And when a child learns of space travel, discussion concerns whether, if he so travels, regardless of what he learns, will he be older or younger than his stay-at-home brother when he returns" (private communication, 1995).

7. *Quest to sustain paradox*:
    a. "Over the years Milner struggled with the question of blankness of background, i.e., whether the basic idea is get back to the satisfied dreamlessness of the infant at the breast after a feeding, or whether this blankness of background is not also the conscious mind perceiving its own unconscious processes" (Scott, 1975c, p. 317). Scott added that it is not just A or B, but both; he then quoted Winnicott, who, referring to the paradox of the transitional object, suggested that the paradox be accepted rather than be resolved, with the resultant loss of its value as paradox.
    b. There are various types of confusion: confusion between ego and object; good and bad objects; heterosexual and homosexual objects; and regressive and progressive depression. "These types of confusion must be carefully discriminated... if confusion is not to be confounded" (*Mourning and Zest*, pp. 145-146).

8. *Incongruous measurements and incongruous sequencing of events*:
    a. "Scientists publish so much that Oppenheimer has said that if the present rate of publication continues, this literature will outweigh the world within the next century. This points to limits" (Scott, 1964b, p. 3).
    b. "Our hands handle, and our mouths mouth, our cocks and cunts piss, or with boys our pissers piss, but we are soon taught Latin" (Scott, 1986b, p. 10).

c. "As a boy I wondered about *amare*, the Latin word for *love*. The Bible story began with creation and I wondered why Latin began with love" (*Mourning and Zest*, p. 36).

9. *Totalities made by accumulated noises*:
"How many gigs make a giggle" (private communication, 1992)?

10. *Point of view projected into part objects*:
"Children soon argue about the immovable object and the irresistible force. In one way or another they soon discover how hard it is to be conscious of both aspects of a conflict—for instance, when they link their hands and start to pull them apart, and ask themselves: Can I be so strong that I can pull them apart, and yet so strong that I can hold them together?" (Scott, 1964b, p. 1).

11. *The limiting of the limitless*:
a. "Children later ask: 'Can I harness power that can counteract any power? Can I discover everything? Will it just take plenty of time?'" (Scott, 1964b, p. 1).
b. "I ask whether everything (God), or something (which we can give a name to), or nothing, for instance, sleep with a smile, is the most important thing to draw or to talk about. Or is it the link between all three: everything, something and nothing that is the most important" (1990b, p. 9)?
c. The U.S. Marines championed Whitehead's proverb, "The impossible just takes longer" (Scott, 1975c, p. 281).

12. *Combined reflexivity and recursivity*:
Repeatedly Scott spoke of our reflexivity (e.g., awake to being awake) which he combines—with a detectable enjoyment—with recursivity —(e.g., aware of awareness of awareness of forgetting of remembering and remembering it).
a. "We must heed remembering and forgetting, paying attention and reflecting (forgetting, forgetting and remembering, remembering)" (private communication).
b. "We can dream of daydreams, and daydream of dreams of day dreaming about waking and sleeping with or without dreams or remembering them but anticipating others" (private communication).

13. *Reversibility and controvertibility of experience*:
a. "The child breathes out and wonders if he can get it back in" (private communication, 1990).

b. "As a child, I often wondered about the caption in my picture book that read 'When there is nobody with me I am all alone,' and wondered if there were two stories, i.e., whether 'I'm all alone' is the same as 'there's nobody with me'" (*Becoming a Psychoanalyst*, p. 225).

Scott (1985) filtered much of his discourse through the above thirteen categories. Hovering above them is Scott's irony, even self-ironical posture, as when he refered to "the lover who looks at his beloved smiling in her sleep and asks himself, 'Is she smiling at me?'" (p. 33). The reader also meets with Scott's constant curiosity, wonderment, and a particular fascination with beginnings. The poem (*Becoming a Psychoanalyst*, p. 228) ending the first volume of his autobiography, for example, is about his first child's first waking and first movements: a stirring[26] and inklings of a smile. But no sooner had Scott mentioned those initial actions than he spoke of his awe, which he then maximalized in asserting that "there is no greater joy."

I see it fitting to terminate this section by referring to another striking passage that Scott wrote. Remarkable for about how much psychoanalytic wisdom and about how much of psychic life can be condensed into so short an expository space, the passage contains many thematic motifs and categorical matrices (the play of opposites, klang association, maximilization, recursive reflexivity) that are the trademark of Scott's discourse. The reader will also note the serendipitous use of klang associations (mad, sad, glad) in various sequences to portray the course of human experience. The shortness of the rhyming refrain is offset by the amplitude and central importance of its meaning—basic psychic states. And the superficial jingle of the rhyming sequence is undercut by the interaction of its meanings, the transformation of basic psychic states which comprises a crucial difference between healthy and unhealthy life. The one expository fault in the passage below is found in the last sentence, whose last dozen words should be rephrased as "in sharing the sadness rather than becoming potent in sharing the gladness of successful mourning":

> The patient who is sad at having been mad may by progression become mad at being sad. He works with the ambivalence of glad versus mad at being sad until he can tolerate and believe his loved objects can tolerate being glad at being sad on the way to being glad at being glad. Then he can test new reality in mourning without forgetting that the work being done is making reparation. This is perhaps maximally seen in glad sad potency, with tears and laughter mixed, without fear that the partner will become impotent sharing the sadness rather than sharing the potent gladness of successful mourning (Scott, 1984b, p. 154).

V. Scotsland: A Selective Collection of Clinical Vignettes

In his zestful awakenness, Scott was quick to notice unusual clinical phenomena and then to leave a record of them scattered throughout his abundant writings, lectures, and private papers. But he was also alert to the exceptional experience of others, including Winnicott's with a dead patient. It is fitting to begin this last section of the essay with Scott's write-up of his friend Winnicott's moribund surprise: Winnicott "heard that if you inject adrenalin into the heart muscles, the heart would start to beat again. The person would come back to life. He did it. The patient became alive. He looked at both Winnicott and the nurse and said, 'Oh, I thought I died,' and then he died again. Then Winnicott said, 'I'll have to be careful. I don't think I want to do that again'" (Hunter, 1995, pp. 205-206).

We turn now to Scott's own patients. As we journey through that mind scape, we hear many stories with varying unusualness in their subjects, incidents or dialogue, beginning with Scott's anxiety during his very first attempt at hypnosis when his female-subject had problems waking up (*Becoming a Psychoanalyst*, p. 68). We next follow Scott (1952) as he recalls that prior to 1952, he had two patients that somnambulated in the course of their therapeutic interviews (*ibid.*, p. 1). With equal bemusement, Scott further reminisced about naive patients who, when asked to lie down, did so on their stomach and looked at the analyst (Scott, 1970) or they laid with their head at the opposite end of the couch (*ibid.*). Bringing up a stranger case, Scott told of his only patient who could dream backwards and of another who tried with her own eyes to see underneath her own eyelids (private communication, 1992).

From the above short anecdotes we proceed to a series of short sketches which Scott wrote up for us to ponder and savor:

"I was intrigued by the patient using a cane who could not feel his hands on the cane but could feel the object touched by the end of the cane (*Becoming a Psychoanalyst*, p. 215).... In one of my child patients, 'humming' was an attempt to control screaming; he began to ask people if they could 'hum' a scream" (Scott, 1958, p. 3).... I had a child in analysis whose mother described him as being "excited without being excited" (*Becoming a Psychoanalyst*, p. 191).... While strolling with a patient on the hospital grounds, I asked a patient to locate his complaint of his terrible pain, the patient pointed to the top of a flagpole and said,"There it is" (*Becoming a Psychoanalyst*, pp. 215-216).... One of my patients at the Boston Psychopathic Hospital was proud of her capacity to achieve undetected orgasm during interview by sucking the inside of her lower lip (*Becoming a Psychoanalyst*, p. 10 and p. 152); I gave her 500 hours of therapy at the rate of five times a week (*ibid.*, p. 143). Years later she told me: "We tried to do too much too quickly" (*ibid.*, p. 156).... A

problem of a female patient was her belief that "Greta Garbo is me" instead of the reverse, "I am Greta Garbo," which interested me (*ibid.*, p. 210)....
Another patient said that his childhood dreams were between the armoire and his bedroom wall, but when he improved, he recognized that his dreams were in him (*ibid.*, p. 216).... At the end of the war, I had the experience of trying to treat a war-neurosis in a man who was blind, deaf, and dumb, with the aid of a nurse who translated for me (Scott, 1976).... One patient said that she wanted to kill me. But I told her that I'd like to kill her first before she killed me. And then I cried" (private communication, 1980).

From the foregoing series we journey on to the mostly longer vignettes from Scott's fascinating clinical experience.

To read them quickly would cause a blurring effect that would undercut the reader's comprehension. In B.B.C. news broadcasting, let us note, a pause separating each news item enables the listener to better assimilate what he is hearing. Inspired by such sensible communicative practice, I have separated each of Scott's vignettes by linear spacings and a row of asterisks, thereby inviting the reader to reflectively pause for his own benefit:

The first patient I had under Jones was a man whose wife called because he was impotent when he was awake. But he began to play with her in his sleep and he had intercourse with her in his sleep (*Becoming a Psychoanalyst*, pp. 10, 201). Ella Sharpe supervised me as a student with a case of a man with the symptom of being potent only in sleep (Scott, 1975c, p. 309).

* * *

I supervised Khan who had a patient who could read his mind; the case did not succeed because Khan was at a loss. I would have told the patient that he was anxious about submitting to my analyzing him (private communication, 1976).

* * *

I once had a patient who wondered why people forget dreams. He felt he had always remembered all his dreams, but that they were private. From the beginning of analysis he was struck by my interest in everything, including dreams. His associations recurrently led to recent and old dreams, but rarely did he say "I dreamt last night" unless it was a dream he had been preoccupied with since waking. His analysis was the fastest I have ever experienced. We did not discover why he had not forgotten many dreams. The nearest we came to understanding this was to conclude that the continuity of memory of infantile dreams was a substitute for the discontinuity of memory of infantile waking experiences, but why both did not undergo early repression we did not understand (Scott, 1975c, p. 324).

* * *

Once only during psychoanalytic treatment has a patient taken my photograph. I was bored, he was boring and ruminating about sleeping and not remembering dreams. Suddenly he sat up, turned around and said, "Doc, I am going to take your picture," and did so with his Minox. Later he gave me a print. The remainder of the interview dealt with his destructiveness in human relationships and his difficulty in maintaining an image of any constructive desire (Scott, 1975c, p. 329).

* * *

A patient of mine dreamed of being in prison and eventually becoming able to climb up to a high window in the wall and look out onto a country landscape with wonderment. The dreamer woke to find himself leaning dangerously out of a window of a hotel several stories up looking at the landscape he had seen in the dream. He had arrived at the hotel in the dark the night before.

He was suicidal by day. In the dream the landscape was beautiful and he was in prison. He awoke frightened of the danger of falling. If he tried to fly over the beauty he would not fly long but fall and be smashed. He experienced the nothing between and death on waking. Between sleep and dream and waking the gap was filled with a memory of a dream of mother, of waking without mother being there, and the vague confusion of what was the transformation from the dream of mother to the nothing (Scott, 1986c, p. 27).

* * *

A depersonalized spinster complained of never being awake like others. She felt most awake in pitch darkness. A male patient, on the other hand, complained that he could not wake as he used to—like snapping his fingers. Now the world was "spotted" with his dreams. In sessions he was sleepy but said he could not sleep unless I slept first (Scott, 1975c, p. 256).

* * *

A female patient could never understand how anyone could ever be like anyone else. I pointed out that and related feelings "were partial memories of an infantile situation in which, while feeding, she felt that the balance of eating her way into her mother, in contrast to eating and taking her mother inside herself, had shifted in the direction of eating her way into her mother in order to find a nipple inside. Such fantasies of being inside extend to being inside the mother's nipple and breast" (Scott, 1975c, pp. 313-314).

* * *

For a year and a half I watched a female patient who had tight lips, rounded tongue, with frequent movements of the tongue slightly out of the mouth, combined with anxieties about talking nonsense. When her fear of blathering now in infancy, due to her mother's rejection of it as a libidinal activity were interpreted, she pleasurably blathered three or four times. In my interpretation I did not speak the word blathering; I made the movement and sound which had a crucial effect. I said "You went (I blathered) to your mother and wanted her to blather (I blathered) to you." She smiled and blathered three or four cycles; she began to stammer; she was frightened lest she continue to stammer. Within two weeks she described the situation that had occurred in analysis, as she had wished it had happened in childhood. She said "I showed you something and you did it too." During the treatment it had only been after eighteen months that I was able to imagine that this was what she wanted to do (Scott, 1953b, pp. 3-4; 1984a, pp. 459-460).

Her other symptoms included longstanding fears of being alone and of vomiting or seeing anyone vomit. Toward the end of the analysis, the fear of vomiting abated and she had a pleasant dream of vomiting into a cupped breast; also toward the end of the analysis, the fear of being alone abated as I analyzed her omnipotent fantasies of being the whole world and of being inside her mother who herself was identified with the world (Scott, 1976b, p. 3).

* * *

Mr. B's problem was that of trying to express a great deal in very little and that little poetically. He had an earlier belief that the stars were holes in heaven and that one star represented the place from which he had come and through which he would return... This feeling of his was related not only to fantasies of what it was like before birth, but in infancy, to the difficulty in solving the problem of where was mother—was she outside, was she beside, or was he inside, and was she multiple or single? After much analysis, this ended with a short poem:

The problem is not to find the needle
In the haystack
The problem is
Where to put it (Scott, 1977, p. 11).

* * *

After several years of analysis Mrs. G. was still depressed, especially because she could not have any feeling of union in her love for her husband. After several more years she overcame this difficulty and expressed the feeling that her love was so great that she wished to become the man she loved and wanted him to love her so much that he would wish to be her. These feelings preceded her discovery and fusion in lovemaking (Scott, 1977, p. 15).

* * *

One patient decided, as he put it, "Most of your patients are crazy and lie on the couch, I am going to lie on the floor." He did so with his feet a foot or so away from the foot of my chair. He continued so for two years until he eventually rose and sat facing me (Scott, 1970, p. 8).

* * *

From time to time I have collected individual responses to listening to white noise. The person talks without being able to hear what he is saying, as the white noise masks his own voice.... With my female patient (who had eleven personalities) I wondered how much her hate was of hearing her voice expressing hate and how much it was kinesthesia of the action of expressing hate vocally. In other words, when she was sadistic the pleasure may have been in the activity and the hate in the sound which she was putting in to the other person. The kinesthesia and the sound may be separated by masking the hearing of her voice with white sound recording speech which can be heard later (Scott, 1989, p. 19).

* * *

A patient became silent after discussing a newly acquired panoramic view of his childhood, feeling that there was much more than he could ever speak of. He then clicked his right thumb-nail on one of the finger-nails of his right hand, but did not make a sound which I could hear. When it was interpreted that, as a defense against his inability to talk fast enough to say what he wanted to say, he had tried the opposite, namely, to discover how small a noise he could make with his nails, he quickly said that he was just about to describe a fantasy of bouncing on the couch like a baby but was afraid by my interpretation about something he couldn't control. His response showed the partial incorrectness of my interpretation, which should have included mention of the small controlled movement as well as the small controlled sound. He regressed to a bouncing baby instead of to a bouncing, yelling baby (Scott, 1958, pp. 3-4).

* * *

A patient who was a piano player told me that when playing with one hand and masturbating with the other, he felt that if he played with two hands, he would risk a spontaneous orgasm and would not be able to play with an éclat equal to the orgasm (Scott, 1987a, p. 13).

* * *

I had a woman in analysis who undressed and tried to dance and sing triumphantly the song "I don't need psychoanalyzing, I'm just in love." I wondered if she would get dressed or was she going to embarrass me. She did dress before the end of the interview (Hunter, 1995, pp. 202-203).

* * *

The youngest child I ever analyzed was the supervisory case of a 26-month-old boy I had with Klein: He came because he wasn't speaking, and I only analyzed him for nine months because he began to speak so quickly and so rapidly, though he never spoke to me. I carried the analysis on quite some time until he could speak understandably to others. He understood me, but he didn't speak (Scott, 1976a, p. 8). At the sixth interview the boy imitated the father humping in the primal scene (Scott, 1984b). The only words he spoke in analysis were "mum" and "Baba" (his teddybear); he yelled in rage once and made a few sounds during the sessions. Once he stood in the middle of the room, looked alertly about and yelled as loudly as he could. He then was silent for a moment, listening attentively and when nothing happened he broke into a beautiful smile. I did not discover how much his showing me his feelings about parental intercourse and not making a sound about what he showed, even though I talked about it; he was only showing me what he actually felt when he was observing parental intercourse and how much it was revenge at the parent-analyst of the parents not talking to him about their intercourse which he not only hated but also blessed (Hunter, 1995, p. 191; Scott, 1975a, p. 293).

* * *

Under the analytic exploration of the effect of interpreting [Mrs. B's] fear of discovering a link, while awake or asleep, between the love she had discovered for her previous therapist and her inhibited orgastic activity she eventually dreamt, "I had an orgasm and shrieked with delight." . . . As we sought links between the dream and its functional and objectless pleasure on the one hand, and her transient pleasure with and for men and meanwhile depreciating them as not good enough, often because of their other commitments more or less secret to her, she began to become angry at me for having, as she said, stolen her dream. She said that analysis was dishonest... Later her murderous anger at me led to my having to interpret and confront her with the fact, that if she murderously attacked me, I would defend myself and hope that I could control her, or kill her first, as I valued myself more than I valued her, but that I was very sad that all the work we had done which had accomplished so much for her, was in danger of being destroyed by her... She could not tolerate distinguishing me from herself, her pleasure, her shriek, her talk, etc. Her dream was a turning point in her analysis and was more useful than had she spontaneously or in some response to an interpretation screamed orgasticallly with delight during an interview (Scott, 1986c, pp. 23-24).

* * *

The intensity of feeling may spread to the secret joy of a noisy orgasm involving a patient who told of a famous singer falling more in love with her than he had ever been before. He told her he could not love her without being able to risk singing which would not be heard by more than them. She borrowed a house on a moor miles from anywhere. Not only did he sing but, as she said, bellowed telling the world defiantly "I love and I'm loved" but at the same time keeping all their love a secret to themselves on the moor (Scott, 1986c, p. 25).

* * *

Another patient complained of not being able to be one with anyone she loved. The hope for this oneness was lost and she was depressed. The only hope she felt was in my hope. Eventually, she believed oneness could be obtained only if she loved someone she wanted to be. Nevertheless, this would not suffice unless he also wanted to be her. Then they could come together, become one, and separate later and tolerate the disillusionment.... In the background of memory was the fact that objects subjected her to being subjected at the same time that she, as a subject, had objected to objects being objects (Scott, 1986c, p. 25).

* * *

Sometimes one of my male patients "relaxed so much that he snored so much when he was awake." Sometimes after snoring he would say immediately that he had been so relaxed and blank that he had snored, but had not slept. In other interviews we inferred that he had slept and dreamt that he had been awake blank, relaxed, and that he had snored as sometimes he told me he had snored when I had not heard him... He was also either passive with regard to waking up (he woke immediately [after] I spoke) or unconscious of waking up. When I interpreted that the psychoanalytic situation was so allied to his feelings of the feeding situation that he was not separating them, he became conscious of the fact that he could neither have a phantasy nor a memory of the situation he was in (he had no sensations of his body on the couch when he became blank)—he began to realize how very blank the blankness had been... I connected his talk of thinking (his thoughts are very much inside) and his talk of feeling (feelings to him are mostly something other people have) with the split he had made between thinking and feeling between the mouth and the nipple... His associations were to his hiding breast memories behind his intellect—to wondering whether thinking is like a cow ruminating to anger at not being able to enjoy pleasure in psychoanalysis—to anger at my not giving him the pleasure he would have liked his mother to have given him—to his wanting me to make use of his productions as he would have liked his mother to have appreciated his sucking (Scott, 1952, p. 2).

* * *

Mrs. A was very depressed and could talk very little. She said there was something she wanted to say but she could not remember and could not understand why she had forgotten. Several decades ago, for the one and only time in my practice, I tried to see if this state of affairs would be changed by giving her a few breaths of nitrous oxide (laughing gas)—just enough to produce sleep.... On repeated occasions when she woke she began to smile almost childishly and as she woke to where she was she said two things: "I'll never tell you that... I'll never remember that." She then startled momentarily and became the depressed person she had previous been, forgetting what she had said.

The only other parameter I used during her treatment was one long interview, hoping that she might go to sleep in the interview. The interview lasted twelve hours. She did not sleep and it was no different from twelve consecutive hours. The interview was held in her own home (Scott, 1986c, pp. 22-23).

* * *

A female patient jumped up very suddenly from her stupor, intending to throw herself through the window, which was beyond the foot of the couch. Luckily, at that moment, I was alert enough to catch her leg. She fell on the floor beyond the couch and I fell on the couch. The only comparable experience I had was with a patient in analysis in hospital who was sitting up on the couch lighting a cigarette. Without warning, she set fire to her hair. I did not wait for her to put it out—I used my hands (Scott, 1970, p. 4).

* * *

A child I know said: "I do not want to die. I like it here." He spent several days testing people out to find out if he could find someone who would tell him that there was somebody in the world who had lived forever.... It took him some time to believe that he could not go back; he had to go on and on, and try to make-up in some way for lost chances and for the loss of the belief that he could live backwards, or could go to sleep and wake up yesterday. He came to believe he would always wake up tomorrow (Scott, 1986c, pp. 20-21).

* * *

A drowsy patient in a drowsy way said: "I guess I'd better believe I am not everything" then he started and asked me in a clear voice: "Did I say, I guess I'd better believe I am not everything?" I said: "Yes." . . . he was giving up the belief in his omnipotent idealized wishes to be everything, to do everything, and to have everything done for him magically, just because he could wish. He could say, "I am what is inside me. I am not what is outside me." Perhaps the simplest way to put this disillusionment is to say that consciousness or waking are no longer identical with creativity (Scott, 1984b, pp. 152-153; 1986c, pp. 26-27).

I close this inventory of clinical vignettes with an excerpt from one of the periodic telephone calls that Dr. Scott and I have had together. He referred to his supervision of an aborted analysis in which the patient, a female stand-up comic, defensively used her talent to keep her candidate-analyst laughing anytime she wanted.

I replied: "What if a patient had the combined talents of a stand-up (or lie-down) comic and a telepathist who could read the analyst's mind?"

And he said with a laugh, "It's too much." And I then thought to myself, "By scot, it's much too much..."

NOTES

1. Two undated entries in the concluding bibliography merit mention here, as I shall have occasion to refer to them. Scott's lengthy monograph, *Mourning and Zest*, remains unpublished; on the other hand, the first volume of his autobiography, *Becoming a Psychoanalyst*, has been accepted by Free Associations Press. At present, Scott is working on the other two volumes of his autobiographical project. Because Scott's syntactical control is often wanting, I have not hesitated to make silent minor changes in quoting him; in no case, however, have I dared to alter meaning.

2. I might add that Freud never used the term "fall-to sleep-work" (*Einschlafarbeit*). All subsequent footnotes continue my commentary on the main text.

3. Elsewhere Scott speaks of children's frustration about wanting to walk ahead alone and yet wanting simultaneously to talk about that experience to the person they have left behind (*Mourning and Zest*, 224).

4. You may wake up with a dream-high or a dream-over from having one too

many dreams, all of those residues possibly containing anticipations of dreaming, waking up, sleeping, remembering and forgetting.

5. *Wacharbeit* (G.W.: 2/3, pp. 578, 594), the German term for "wake-work," was translated by Strachey respectively as "the activity of waking life" and "waking activity" (Freud, 1900, pp. 573, 589).

6. It takes further wake-work to distinguish between a sleep-wake, a dream-wake, a daydream-wake, a wake-up from hallucination, and an hallucinated wake.

7. We also need to know the bearing of that connection upon "wancies" or what might be labeled as fantasies about waking.

8. In that we are never fully awake, we're "awaking" during the day, mindless that part of our minds sleeps on: we go to sleep, then wake the other part of ourselves up to dream, then wake up but not to sleepwalk but to dream-walk and dream-talk. Day in and day out, thus we lead our awaking lives. Recalling his early technique with Miss Lucy, Freud (1893-1895) said that it was possible to "re-awaken, after an interval of twenty-one years," details of an experience in her "who, in fact, was in a waking state" (2, p. 114 fn.).

9. In this context we should know that in Sanskrit, Buddha means the awakened or illuminated one. It is quite to the point that it was he who founded the founder of the world's oldest mystical tradition. The Greek etymology of *mystic*, "to close the eyes," lends an interlingual aptness to the fact that statues of Buddha the mystic often present him in an awakened state, yet with his eyes closed.

10. Etymologically, dreaming in German means to deceive; and in Hebrew, to have orgasm; philologically therefore, in Hebrew, a wet dream is a tautology. The dream poaches wilfully on the reserve of our internalizations; while some of them are left to sleep, others are summoned to strut in the spotlight or strobe lights of our night mind. One could say that by thinking that dreams of neurotics do not differ from each other (Freud, 1915-1917, p. 456), Freud posits an incidental similarity between dreams and death, the great leveler. One is reminded of de Gaulle's sad relief at the burial of his Mongoloid daughter: "*Maintenant* elle est comme les autres" (She is *now* like the others).

11. Although monks in their solitude choose to withdraw from the world, their ascetic lack of sleep counters the withdrawal of cathexes upon the self.

12. In *The Interpretation of Dreams* Freud (1900) alluded to a special capacity of some dreamers: "There are some people who are quite clearly aware during the night that they are asleep and dreaming and who thus seem to possess the faculty of consciously directing their dreams" (p. 571). On the next page Freud quoted an author who had "acquired the power of accelerating the course of his dreams... and of giving them any direction he chose. It seems as though in his case the wish to sleep had given place to another precon-

scious wish, namely to observe his dreams and enjoy them." But as Freud
privately admitted to Fliess, he himself could direct his dreams, but he dared
not say that publicly for fear of undermining the scientific stature of his
Dreambook.

13. Dreaming occasions an awakening of consciousness, and secondary revision
occasions a further awakening (cf. Freud, 1900, p. 575).

14. Since a dream aims not to be understood by its dreamer, it does not have a
communicative function; and if successful, the dream has but a transitional
representational function. The reporting of dreams, of course, can be enlisted
as a defense against sleeping and dreaming in analytic sessions.

15. I am unfamiliar with anyone reporting an exact or telescoped anniversary
phenomenon in remembering a sleep or dream from hours to years after-
wards.

16. The manner of telling a dream may be mimetic of its symbolic form. At other
times, the manner of narration, such as a dreamy drift into telling or a sleepy
telling, may have more to do with the overall dream as an act that ended too
soon.

17. To say it more poetically, in the ballet of diurnal and nocturnal chiaroscuro,
the shadow of the daydream falls upon the dream, and the night light of the
dream falls upon the daydream.

18. According to Freud's dispersed sartorial associations, when going to sleep,
we undress both our body and mind (1917, p. 222) and strip ourselves of our
morality garments (1915, p. 286)—to avoid hurtful redress, we might add as
a punful condensation. Our dreams then take on a clothing disguise (*Traum-
verkleidung*, G.W., 2/3, pp. 519, 520, 618; Freud, 1900, pp. 515, 613). I have
often observed that a prominent color in a patient's dream matches the color
of his clothing, thus indicating that when dressing in the morning he is
unconsciously continuing his dream. For another thing, nakedness, just like
clothing, might also be a cover-up.

19. Accordingly, psychoanalysis "denaturalizes" dreams into being first remembered, and then understood. In that the best functioning dream is that
which is not remembered, it is a dream-slip, a fall-out in mental ecology, that
lies at the root at the discovery of psychoanalysis. Whatever its royalty, the
road to the unconscious is a potted, defective one.

20. It would be more accurate to say that the patient's statement just prior to the
reported dream is his first association to it.

21. Is there any study of the kinds of dreams of those people who dream with
eyes open or half closed? Note that in Greek one can say, "I *saw* a dream."
Such visuality is lost in other languages. Cf. English: "I had a dream";
French, "I made a dream" (*j'ai fait un rêve*); German: it has dreamt to me (*es
hat mir geträumt*).

22. An example of Scott's own discriminatory perceptiveness of infantile

behavior is found in an experiment that he urged Winnicott to carry out. The latter "watched babies of six to twelve months sitting on their mothers' laps while he sat across the corner of his desk from them. He placed a metal tongue depressor on the empty corner of the table and described the states of the baby's reaction to the new object; from the various ways of taking the object, to the various ways of playing with it during mounting oral excitement, until it was played with enough and was dropped, and either retrieved or neglected. The modification I proposed was: as soon as the baby takes the tongue depressor one also takes hold of it and gently holds it until the baby lets go, and then immediately replaces it where it was before. Once can then observe whether the baby is frustrated or disappointed, and if disappointed, how he mourns the lost object or opportunity and makes up (reparation); (a) by using a new opportunity to play with it again or, (b) by seeking a substitute object" (1982b, p. 154). Scott called such an experiment a test of "micro-grief" and "the work of micro-mourning" (*Mourning and Zest*, p. 107).

23. In consultations I also question about minimal experience, e.g., when were you least guilty or how can you imagine becoming least guilty.

24. The constraints of Western social conventions being what they are, we should bear in mind that the less people know each other—and a fortiori on the occasion of their first meeting—the less will they resort to noise as a vocal exchange. Contrarily, the more people know each other, the more will they utter noises in informal settings, and most especially in circumstances both of erotic intimacy and of waking up together.

25. I suggest the term "otomization" for this phenomenon.

26. One of Freud's most principal technical terms is *Regung*, meaning stirring or the beginning of a movement; in Freud's original German texts, for instance, we come across hundreds of times such composites as wish-stirrings or instinctual stirrings. That fact that Strachey mistranslates *Regung* as "impulse" or "excitement" has caused it to be unfortunately unappreciated by English readers—unfortunately because usually we direct our clinical sensitivity not to obvious excitation but rather to the subtler stirrings. The phenomenon of firstness, of course, leads us into the problematic question of origins which baffled Freud all his life. I am reminded of the story told by Erikson about his being lost in Vermont, then asking a farmer for directions to a certain town and getting the reply: "If I wanted to go where you wanted to go, I wouldn't start from here."

REFERENCES

Freud, S. (1893-1895). *Studies on Hysteria. SE*, 2, 1955. In: J. Strachey (Ed.), *Standard Edition of the Complete Psychological Works of Sigmund Freud*, 24 volumes. London: Hogarth Press and The Institute of Psycho-Analysis, 1953-1974.

Freud, S. (1900). *Interpretation of Dreams. S.E.*, 4 &5, 1953. [*Gesammelte Werke*, 2/3, Frankfurt a/M.: Fischer Verlag, 1942.]

—— (1901). *Psychopathology of Everyday Life. SE*, 6, 1960.

—— (1915). Thoughts for the times on war and death. *SE*, 14, 1957, pp. 275-300.

—— (1915-1917). *Introductory Lectures on Psychoanalysis. SE*, 15 & 16, 1961.

——(1917). A metapsychological supplement to the theory of dreams. *SE*, 14, 1957, pp. 222-235.

—— (1925). Some additional noes on dream-interpretation as a whole. *SE*, 19, 1961, pp. 125-138.

—— (1940). *An outline of psychoanalysis. SE*, 23, 1964, pp. 141-207.

Hunter, V. (1995). An interview with Clifford Scott. *Psychoanal. Rev.*, 82: 189-206.

Rey, H. (1992). Awake, going to sleep, asleep, dreaming, awaking, awake: Comments on W. Clifford Scott. *Free Assns.*, 3: 439-454.

Scott, C. (1948a). A psychoanalytic concept of the origin of depression. *Br. Med. J.*, 1: 1-9.

—— (1948b). Some embryological neurological psychiatric and psychoanalytic implications of the body scheme. *Int. J. Psycho-Anal.*, 29: 141-152.

—— (1952). Patients who sleep or look at the psychoanalyst during treatment – Technical considerations. *Int. J. Psycho-Anal.*, 33: 1-5.

—— (1953a). A new hypothesis concerning the relationship of libidinal and aggressive instincts based on clinical evidence obtained chiefly during the treatment of patients with manic-depressive illnesses (unpublished lecture, delivered at the International Psychoanalytic Congress, London, July 29).

—— (1953b). A note on blathering. *Int. J. Psycho-Anal.*, 36: 3-4.

—— (1958). Noise, speech and technique. *Int. J. Psycho-Anal.*, 39: 1-4.

—— (1960). Symposium on "depressive illness": III. Depression, confusion and multivalence. *Int. J. Psycho-Anal.*, 41: 497-503.

—— (1962). Symposium: A reclassification of psychopathological states. *Int. J. Psycho-Anal.*, 53, 344-350.

—— (1964a). Mania and mourning. *Int. J. Psycho-Anal.*, 45: 373-377.

—— (1964b). The limitations of science. *Canad. Med. Assn. J.*, 91: 700-703.

—— (1970). A review of the psychoanalytic situation (unpublished lecture, delivered at the Canadian Psychoanalytic Society, Montreal, November 19).

—— (1974). Self envy and envy of dreaming (unpublished lecture, delivered at the Canadian Psychoanalytic Society, Montreal, May 23).

—— (1975a). Comments on Freud's views about sleep (unpublished lecture, delivered at the Canadian Psychoanalytic Society, Montreal, January 23).

—— (1975b). Discussion of Dr. Knapp's paper (unpublished commentary, delivered at the Canadian Psychoanalytic Society, Montreal, April 17).

Scott, C. (1975c). Remembering sleep and dreams (title of the whole issue of *Int. Rev. Psycho-Anal.*, 2: 253-354, containing twelve essays by Scott).

—— (1976a). Discussion of Dr. Mahony's paper (unpublished commentary, delivered at the Canadian Psychoanalytic Society, Montreal, June 10).

—— (1976b). Two recorded interviews (unpublished lecture, delivered at the Canadian Psychoanalytic Society, Toronto, March 10).

—— (1977). Notes on conscious and unconscious conflicts in the transference (unpublished lecture, delivered at the Canadian Psychoanalytic Society, Montreal, June 16).

—— (1978a). Common problems concerning the views of Freud and Jung. *J. Anal. Psychol.*, 23: 303-312.

—— (1978b). Discussion of Dr. Fayek's paper (unpublished commentary, delivered at the Canadian Psychoanalytic Society, Montreal, Nov. 23).

—— (1981a). Discussion of Dr. Lakoff's paper (unpublished commentary, delivered at the Canadian Psychoanalytic Society, Montreal, February 19).

—— (1981b). The development of the analysands' and analysts' enthusiasm for the process of psychoanalysis. In: J. S. Grotstein (Ed.), *Do I Dare Disturb the Universe?*, Beverly Hills: Caesura Press, pp. 571-577.

—— (1982). Melanie Klein: 1882-1960. *Psychia. J. Univ. Ottawa*, 7: 149-157.

—— (1984a). Primitive mental states in clinical psychoanalysis. *Contemp. Psychoanal.*, 20: 458-463.

—— (1984b). Psychoanalysis of a boy of 26 months with a 20 year follow-up (unpublished lecture, delivered at the Canadian Psychoanalytic Society, Montreal, October 24).

—— (1985). Narcissism, the body, phantasy, fantasy, internal and external objects and the "body scheme." *J. M. Klein Soc.*, 3: 23-48.

—— (1986a). Mourning, the analyst, and the analysand. *Free Assn.*, 7: 7-10.

—— (1986b). The broken links between sleep and the unconscious and waking and the conscious (unpublished lecture, delivered at the Canadian Psychoanalytic Society, Montreal, May 22).

—— (1986c). Who is afraid of Wilfred Bion? (unpublished lecture, delivered to the Canadian Psychoanalytic Society, Montreal, May 22).

—— (1987a). Making the best of a sad job (unpublished lecture, delivered at the British Psychoanalytic Society, October 7).

—— (1987b). Repairing broken links between the unconscious, sleep and instinct, and the conscious (unpublished lecture, delivered at the Queen Elizabeth Hospital, Montreal, November 3).

—— (1988). Book reviews of Nini Herman's *My Kleinian Home* (Free Association Books, 1988) and *Why Psychotherapy?* (Free Association Books, 1987). *Free Assns.*, 13: 141-147.

—— (1989). Notes on an example of dissociated personalities without amnesia, with "further notes" (unpublished lecture, delivered at the Canadian Psychoanalytic Society, Montreal, May 18).

Scott, C. (1990a). Hypnosis, sleep and wake, conscious and unconscious (unpublished lecture, delivered at the Canadian Psychoanalytic Society, Montreal, January 18).

—— (1990b). Pictures, music, dreams and creativity (unpublished lecture, delivered at the Queen Elizabeth Hospital, Montreal, October 2).

—— *Mourning and Zest–Mourning and Melancholy* (unpublished mss., 295 pages).

—— (in press). *Becoming a Psychoanalyst.*

1297 St. Viateur
Outremont, P.Q. H2V 1Z2
Canada

JOURNAL OF MELANIE KLEIN AND OBJECT RELATIONS
Volume 15, Number 1, March 1997

ON THE IMITATION OF HUMAN SPEECH

Michael Ian Paul

An exploration of the distortion and misuse of verbal communication is developed with special reference to the imitation of human speech. The problems associated with the thinning and lysis of an encapsulated autistic state are considered with emphasis on the discovery of painful affects. The process of the communication associated with living-in-a-capsule and speaking as though true symbolic communication was occurring with the analyst is considered. The transformation from this primitive state to a state of mind in which sincere authentic communication is possible is discussed. Clinical material is presented to show some of the difficulties involved in the disordered thinking that leads to imitation speech. Special emphasis is placed on the use of an induced fixed state of mind which can take many forms. These inducers organize a "time arrested" phantasied state related to a prenatal phantasy and are used as a part of the barrier to contact with reality.

KEY WORDS: Encapsulation; Barrier; Imitation; Speech; Prenatal; Induced affects; Virtual phantasy; Lysis; Halucinosis; and Simulation.

I

I want to describe a series of structures which can have infinite variation yet have constantly conjoined qualities. In so doing, I wish to set out the main points of this communication that will be fleshed out subsequently:

1. There can be a barrier which separates the patient from true contact with the analyst. This barrier is maintained rigidly although it is subtle.

2. The patient does not engage in true object relations but appears to. The difference between true and false contact can be observed through qualities of the patient's speech. Speech is used as a form of action.

JOURNAL OF MELANIE KLEIN AND OBJECT RELATIONS, 1997, 15(1), 51-76

Sensation rather than meaning is achieved. Speech is used concretely.

3. A barrier to contact disguises a hallucinatory world born of intolerance to frustration. These hallucinatory images have a fixed quality or stereotypy which determines the patient's emotional state. I liken these fixed fantasy states to virtual reality and call them virtual fantasies. They are usually known by the patient and are carefully protected as they offer a sense of security, safety from uncertainty, and a belief in "self-control."

4. When the analyst's interpretations fail to reify the image the patient has in mind, a barrier is erected by the patient. The interpretations are stopped by the barrier and transformed to sensation rather than meaning.

5. Lysis of the barrier results in extreme disorientation while "orientation" means the presence of the system of virtual fantasies remaining in place.

6. When the barrier is breached, certain changes occur similar to the emergence from a prenatal state. Dizziness, the sensation of cold, disorientation, and sensations of extreme pressure attend the lysis of the barrier. These phenomena are linked to phantasies associated with birth.

7. When these disturbing emotions can be tolerated, growth can occur. The barrier to input from the external world is opened when the pain associated with the lysis of the barrier can be understood without automatic withdrawal.

8. I am using the notion of imitative speech to refer to something which sounds like speech but is not communicating symbolic meaning. Rather this form of speech is used to maintain the barrier just described and to induce replicable hallucinatory fantasies.

Much has been discussed recently about autism, from descriptions of the "phenomena in children" to the recognition that there is such an entity in adults. The confusional versus encapsulated forms have been differentiated and described by Frances Tustin (1981), and a less well known post obsessional subclinical form has been described by Donald Meltzer and his co-workers (1975).

In earlier work (1989, 1993) I described some of the clinical findings related to the difficulties encountered in the recognition of imitative speech, or mimesis, in that the imitation in these individuals is an imitation of human speech itself. The problem emerges when one attempts an interpretive intervention using articulate speech and attempts to address the interpretation to a precise point and finds that the analysand is speaking a different language, one which has at its base an action component rather than a symbolic meaning.

From the analysand's unconscious point of reference, the problem involves giving a response which "seems" like the real thing so that the incoming interpretation can be intercepted before registration. This blockade maintains the phantasy of the hermetic seal or encapsulated barrier. This maneuver is meant to give the listener the impression of a satisfactory response. Upon further investigation, the analyst finds that there is no change, only seeming cooperation. So far, all of these considerations are familiar.

In the encapsulated autism described by Tustin (1981) and Meltzer (1975), there has been a cursory discussion of the lack of development of symbolic language. Bion (1955, 1970) described the use of language in psychotic patients as a form of action bypassing meaning. He postulated that the formation of language was integrally related to the establishment of the depressive position. Whole object relations are hindered in relation to the deficit in the development and use of symbolic language. In this article, I explore adult patients who fit the description of Meltzer's subclinical autism and who utilize language as a form of action leading to a failure in development.

In "Language and the Schizophrenic" (1955), Bion sketches the stages of recognition of psychotic states in reference to the use of language. He further elaborates the effects of the "meaningless" but action-oriented communication in *Attention and Interpretation* (Bion, 1970). The practical problem there is the following.

A. The patient behaves as though he were in an encapsulated state with a semi-permeable barrier interposed between the outside world and himself.

B. Both the analyst and analysand are using articulate speech differently, the analyst to communicate meaning, that is to say using language having precise reference in which the words and phrases refer specifically to something. The analysand must block the contact, recognizing the "intent" to communicate, by the analyst's incoming language, which to him means to penetrate the barrier and either stop or change the experience.

C. The patient, as Bion (1970) reminds us, mistakes feeling pain for suffering it. Frustration and intense pain are equated. Pain is sexualized and thereby experienced as inflicted or accepted but not suffered—no meaning develops and a failure of mental growth occurs. Learning is confused with increasing skill at recognizing incoming experience soon enough to deflect it.

D. This experience of the deflected communication is often very sensuous and intense and repeated endlessly as the contact may produce intense sensations which can be sexualized.

E. In Bion's (1970) model, the patient feels the pain of an absence of fulfillment of his desires (to have whatever he has in mind). The absent fulfillment is experienced as a no-thing, and the emotion aroused by the no-thing is felt as indistinguishable from the no-thing. The emotion is, replaced by a no-emotion. Bion (1970) continues, "In practice, this can mean no feeling at all or an emotion such as rage which is a Column 2 emotion, that is an emotion of which the fundamental function is denial of another emotion. As a Column 2 element, all felt emotion is a no-emotion In this respect, it is analogous to 'past' or future as representing the 'place' where the present used to be before all time was annihilated. The place where time was (or feeling was or a no-thing of any kind was) is then similarly annihilated. He continues, "Some patients with which I am familiar achieve a state to which I wish to apply the term non-existence" (p. 20).

F. In Bion's (1970) model, the patient has annihilated time, meaning, symbolic articulate speech and linking associated with violent destructiveness as a function of envy of life itself (presumably in the analyst). There is the destruction of "reality" replaced with the mental detritus resulting from the destruction. Subsequent envy of the life that the object can have becomes a result of the frustration or failure to meet his desires. This summary serves to indicate the state of mind of the patient in order to describe the nature of the receptor to which articulate speech is to be addressed.

Following the abstraction of these desires of the patient for instantaneous reification, there is a wish to be without speech or need for communication. In specific, the patient may say in response to interpretation, "That's not what I had in mind." Further examination reveals a complex set of images (visual or otherwise) which the patient expects to make real by the utterance of the "precise interpretation" which can never approximate to what they have in mind. The expectation by the analysand is that the verbal productions of the analyst are supposed to reify in perpetuity the deeply held phantasy/expectation carried in mind by the analysand. The certainty of frustration and failure of the analyst to produce this long expected result leads to demeaning hostility and despair. Language has been expected to have a result involving reification as a fulfillment of the patient's desires. In Bion's example, the patient has established limited contact with the analyst and is furious because his delusions or hallucinations are not reified. My patient has not achieved this realization, although he suspects it to be true. Bion (1970) formulates,

> The patient then may be seen as facing a choice; either he may allow his intolerance of frustration to use what might be otherwise a no-thing to become a thought, and so achieve the freedom that Freud (1911) describes or he might use what might be a no-thing as the foundation for a system of hallucinosis" (p. 17).

Bion (1970) continued,

> The word "dog" represents different realizations in scientific inquiry and hallucinosis; but the word "dog" is itself not the same when it is representing a realization in scientific inquiry and an element belonging to the domain of hallucinatory transformations. It is sometimes useful to regard it as analogous to the visual image in a reversible transformation. In the visual image, the marks of a drawing on paper remain unchanged but mean two faces or a vase; similarly, dog may mean dog or god. Hallucinations are not representations. They are things in themselves born of intolerance of frustration and desire" (p. 18).

What happens when desire and fulfillment are the same and the patient lives in a state of mind which one could call hallucinosis which is used as a fixed regulator blockading the input to the mind? The phantasy of the "seal" is retained but in the state of hallucinosis to which I refer, there is psychoanalytic verbal "intercourse" which retains seemingly smooth interaction to response. The elaboration of speech, prepared dreams and especially prepared material as problems to discuss maintain the decoying system so that it appears that a conversation is going on. These practiced maneuvers maintain the "dream-hallucination" unless the psychoanalyst's interpretations reach close to the mark. The patient's rejoinder is frequently, "That isn't what I had in mind." At first, this seemed to me to be a remarkably omniscient expectation and usually was associated with hostility. One finds that the response is literal and refers accurately to the fact that the interpretation is not what is held in mind. "I don't see what you mean" as a response often refers to the failure of the interpretation to yield an image which can be compared to the image the patient has in mind. One can compare the response of a patient who receives the same interpretation and associates to it in context evolving further developed material accessing levels of mind previously unexplored. The patient I am describing now engages in a variety of splitting or distancing maneuvers.

The patient behaves as though the analyst "should be" fused with him. Then he would achieve the match expected, but words ought not to be necessary. The use of language or words indicates space between individuals which must be negotiated. Language is felt to involve grave inadequacies at all times. With the "failure to achieve fusion," the analysand must then keep distance from emotional contact since separateness is hated. This process of quiet hatred and disappointment occurs with the avoidance of contact unnoticed and unsaid by both analyst and analysand. Only when this phenomenon becomes the subject of the analytic interaction do overt defensive maneuvers become evident.

One very subtle defense is the use of a particular sense to divide the attention. While the patient is associating and I am interpreting, he is following the outlines of a door, ceiling tiles, or tracing the pattern of a plant leaf or branch with his eyes. One can feel the thinness of the interaction at that time which aids in interpretation. He is "safe"—no contact or diminished contact has been achieved. If the barrier is discovered and the choice can be made to tolerate the frustration-pain, a sudden change can be observed. Initially, intense emotions including anxiety and sadness can be noted. These emotions can be immediately blocked by a drugging stupor communicable to analyst and analysand both. With persistent interpretation over time, frustration can be tolerated better and yields a new configuration which the patient refers to as disorienting. "Orientation" turns out to be "the addiction to the previously held mind-set organized by a particular phantasy." I analogize the hermetically sealed "oriented closed" prior state of mind to a form of autism in which a timeless state is maintained by a fixed phantasy structure I am remaining deliberately abstract as in my experience the variations of these fixed orienting phantasies are numerous. These phantasies can be borrowed from the culture or internally evolved and are used as a virtual world, quite complex yet predictable. There can be infinite variation in form. The use to which these phantasies are put, then, are to prevent frustration and the experience of loss while maintaining a strong emotional tone "played" by the phantasy by induction. This consistent emotional tone then constitutes the reassuring belief that everything is the same. No change is felt to have occurred except when it is ineluctably obvious. This emotional tone is played to the external world, then, and appears as though it is direct and real.

The following is a clinical example involving what I refer to as a virtual fantasy taken from the ninth year of the analysis of a 42-year-old male mathematician.

Clinical Example

The patient enters, eyes averted, and shoots a quick, glaring glance toward me. I immediately have a momentary suspicion that he is deliberately "up to something." He lies on the couch with a smooth athletic motion. I gradually begin to get a headache and feel numb at the same time. There is a recognizable deterioration in the clarity of my state of mind and suddenly I notice a sense of emotional thinness. The patient states, "I don't know what to say." I interpret that he has been attempting to get rid of me by producing pain in me so I will leave him alone. He agrees and I can feel a change in his attention which intensifies. I have a phantasy that something is about to "happen." As I feel my attention increasing and the pain remit, he begins to cry, which is a very different pattern. He then begins to undergo clonic twitching including arms, legs, and torso in short bursts. This goes on for quite a time. These motions are quite exaggerated while at the same time I have the impression he is attempting either to hide this phenomenon or downplay it. The crying continues with a muffled quality. I interpret, "I think you are seeing something that you feel is very upsetting from which you are attempting to split you and me away from at the same time." The clonic twitching increases and the sobbing intensifies to sickening sounds of extreme pain. I interpret, "You are purposely producing an image which you can hold in mind to induce a specific set of feelings that you can use to avoid any contact with me." There is a silence and a profound sense that the patient has mentally disappeared. He agrees and states that he has been observing a large series of people being strapped into serial electric chairs and electrocuted at once.

This is not the first time this image has been used, and has been part of a script this patient has been developing for a film. He then describes the scene with the same sense of divided attention. I notice an intensifying headache again and a desire to leave the room myself. I interpret as I have had many episodes of this sort of thing, that he feels superior in being able to maintain his images which are by now far more real than anything I might say to him. He agrees. The awareness of a barrier existing between us is quite clear to both of us. His responses do not extend what I interpret but serve to keep me at a considerable distance. This same patient has a variety of similar fantasies which can produce sexual sensations or tears or extreme emotional tension on cue, rather like a "method" actor who can depend on the production of feelings at will by changing the internal image. The patient expresses a predilection for crying and states that he not only feels relief but also enjoys the sensation. He can say this not in direct response to a point-on-point interpretation but only after considerable evidence that he feels I have been sufficiently distanced. We have learned subsequently in the analytic work these emotional tricks were consciously utilized to keep his mother at bay, who is both psychotic (hospitalized for periods of time), had shock treatments, and could be both physically and sexually invasive with him. Space does not permit further elaboration of these dynamics here. I present this example as a means of demonstrating the barrier to contact, the use of imagery, which in this situation appears to be consciously induced although subsequently, years later in the analysis, has been found to be a significant part of a negative maternal transference.

II

In this discussion, I wish to describe some problems in the switch from "virtual reality" to object relations. This emergence is painful and is connected to a series of constantly conjoined phenomena which have a relation to the birth process, especially labor. Disorientation, dizziness, vertigo, and sudden cold associated with intense dread occur when an interpretation is so close that it penetrates and is felt as an intrusion (Paul, 1981). Continued progress leads to more frequent contact, usually hated, in the psychoanalytic sessions with no further reference to outside life being made. Later, one may find that a considerable improvement in the patient's outside life occurs.

Certain consistent problems are related within the group of patients who operate behind an "autistic" barrier. The strategy of a psychoanalytic approach, then, must take up the problems associated with the mental journey beyond this barrier. I shall briefly list them and subsequently elaborate more fully. In the psychoanalytic process, one task is establishing contact with external reality. This process involves movement from the addictive standard, time arresting virtual world in which a barrier exists to "protect" the individual from pain, frustration, and a panoply of other emotions including sadness, loss, disorientation, and uncertainty. The virtual organizing phantasy structures, including auto-stimulation, the forms of which can be infinite, provide a consistent, organized, ordered world of feeling which is used by the patient as an attempt to establish meaning but results in a lack of it. The painful discovery that one's emotions are not to be trusted to reflect the experience of reality can be most disturbing. The use of feeling as an instrument of establishing meaning must be retooled. With each step away from certain virtual, established experience, painful affect evolves as previously stated. The autistic barrier "protects" the time arresting virtual phantasy which produces reassuring belief that no change can occur. The effect of establishing a breach in the barrier results in experiences similar to the labor process and emergence from a prenatal state. The "disorientation" described indicates movement away from the "security" of this prenatal state.

In the analytic work, care must be taken to detail the understanding of the anatomy of this virtual world. The components of the virtual phantasy structure need consistent, repeatable, immediate elaboration in order to "work." The work of establishing the morphology and function of these phantasies is met with intense resistance from archaic superego sources as previously described (Paul, 1989). This resistance is in the service of the maintenance of the barrier. As this to and fro of foray out of capsular mental life to uncertainty and painful disorientation can be allowed, there develops a gradual understanding of stereotypic attack blockade from primitive superego sources. The analysand not only gains confidence based on understanding but becomes a collaborator with the analyst when the price of the maintenance of this virtual world is recognized and gradually worked through. The demonstration that the virtual world produces exciting sensation rather than meaning is crucial to the work. Otherwise, the pull to mental masturbatory phantasies as a way of life is too great to tolerate the grief which occurs when the time arresting function is less active. As a psychoanalyst, one has the problem of the analysand's deeply held belief that their virtual experience is the "truth." One problem is that interpretations by the patient emerging from archaic internal sources carry the belief that the only escape from the depression induced by the cruel mutilation of the personality has only been "cured" or substituted for by the deployment of this virtual world. The patient fears being left with nothing. This repetition pattern maintains a profound immaturity and incapacity for the toleration of pain and frustration and subsequently leads to continued reliance on auto-stimulatory mechanisms.

The reader will recognize the instrumental quality of the logic employed by the analysand. Inhibition of the deployment of the virtual world leads to severe emotional pain. Therefore, *"stop everything"* becomes the paradigm for "control" or being in control. Further reactivation of the virtual phantasy occurs with relief from the certain pain resulting from allowing frustration to form the basis of thought. The patient believes that the pain resulting from the restraint leading to thought is the cause of pain. Change in this mechanism threatens the individual's belief in their sanity and is experienced as hurling them into chaos. Thinking is felt to lead to catastrophic experience and is experienced "correctly" as the disorganizing process. The organization which is altered by thinking is the virtual phantasy linked to encapsulation.

The process of development from maintenance of the transmission of psychic experience with the virtual (as if) phantasy in place to contact with the outside directly is exceedingly slow. Paradoxically, change when experienced is very rapid but cannot be tolerated and leads to an abrupt interruption and breakdown of communication with reintroduction of extreme concretism (puns, literal interpretations of obviously complex experience, sometimes quite violently). There are similarities to the negative therapeutic reaction which may mimic envy or extreme hostility, but this attack is employed to stop the communication and the attendant severe anxiety initiated by contact.

Gradually the analysand begins to tolerate the sadness, depression, and intense, psychic pain which I believe is very primitive, perhaps like the experience of a "load" of current being passed through too small a conductor. The intensity of this "pain" can be so great as to bring forth an infantile state of pain prior to verbal thought (either a function of the deployment of the depressive position or the very earliest pain prior to verbal thought). The point I wish to emphasize is that the patient's conscious cooperation in not employing the conscious elements of the virtual addictive phantasy leads to this extremely painful state of affairs. Continuing the analytic process requires a very deep trust in the analyst's capacity to tolerate and suffer the pain benignly. At the same time the analysand has developed the ability to recognize and oppose propaganda which would have automatically established the blockade leading to the maintenance of the phantasy. This complex form of cooperation can only be approached when F (Faith) (Bion, 1970) is strengthened enough to allow for the exposure.

During the time the addictive virtual phantasy is in place, there is a "bottom," a limiting barrier to these painful experiences and communication goes on in a smooth, non-depressed, often quite seemingly interesting but meaningless way. This provides the pleasant, sensuous interchange that can be enjoyable to both analyst and analysand. Typically, the intonation carries the experience in a similar way such that one can note the feeling of importance or perhaps purpose in what appears to sound confident and may indeed be confident as far as the analysand is concerned. Care must be maintained vigilantly that this same pseudo-confidence is not engaged in by the analyst, no matter how tempting. One can see that as the length of time increases that the patient can tolerate life without the addictive phantasy, there is always regret that the old ways gradually lose their appeal. Not only is the pain and depression often intense, but many affects emerge that are experienced as foreign, unknown, strange, and in combinations that have no previous meaning or experience. There is loss of what is perceived as a familiar self on which the analysand has come to depend. There is fear of the vulnerability to experience from the outside which now registers in producing contact with a truer "read" of what is occurring in the external environment. The patient could not have paid "emotional mind" to the experience previously. As a result, "odd" experiences arise; the world that has been fixed in the mind of the analysand by their own design now yields a different experience, usually surprising and not always pleasant. Frequently, those who have been thought to have been friends (by idealization) seem different and yet, upon reflection, there is the increasingly sad realization that one has simply avoided what one knew but dismissed. By contrast, there may be the opposite experience that those who have been maligned may turn out to have been friends. Gratitude is not possible in individuals who have this barrier as acknowledgment of any external contact is too disorienting. "Orientation" describes a reference to the previous link to the virtual addictive phantasy. Gratitude requires the ability to experience something coming into the self from the outside especially in relation to an object.

III

I do not wish to exclude everyday phenomena from orientation to these virtual phantasies. A man buys a computer program to use at home along with a chair that changes attitude, pitch, and yaw, which accompanies visual imagery on a screen simulating the experience of flying a jet fighter. One sees the instruments in the cockpit and, by computerized shifts in the visual display, there are reproducible images generated. These images lead to a mental state in which the sensations, images, and feelings evoked correspond to "slipping into the wind" in an A-10 fighter, simulating each exact step in the landing of the fighter on a moving aircraft carrier. One becomes accustomed to the experience with which the program acquaints one and develops a skill in mastering the configuration of elements necessary to the control of the aircraft during a variety of complex situations which are close enough to real experience as to be of value in training for the real event. One develops skill in maneuvering the virtual aircraft under a variety of circumstances including emergencies which can be programmed to be used in developing experience which would not be available in any other way. This example is a constructive use of a virtual world which reproduces complex mental experiences organized in patterns which gradually achieve familiarity with increasing experience.

Suppose while you are conducting a psychoanalytic session with such a trained individual, you find that they are landing their A-10 Hornet on the deck of a carrier. This subject was not the topic of the conversation. In fact, it was about the anxiety which had occurred reaching quite intense proportions in relation to intense numbness which had arisen while driving to the appointment on the freeway. The numbness and drugged sensation had been so powerful as to raise questions as to the wisdom of pulling off the road and returning home. Only considerable previous experience with this phenomenon has allowed him to understand the organization of this deadened state of mind to cope with the mental pain associated with the emerging feelings under consideration. He knows his intense rage which he has been able to keep to himself was a function of suppression of his frustration and pain at experiencing the penetration of others' painful feeling states. He was at his limit in being able to tolerate them. Being afraid that the analytic contact would lead to greater intensity of feeling, he was able to intercept his ingrained, drugging defense in order to arrive on time to the session. Alternating between oblique, superficial contact and an acknowledgment of his mental state of affairs, I was able to notice and question slight movements of his eyes and body position revealing the various repeated aspects of his simulation of the landing process on a virtual aircraft carrier. This "landing" was going on behind our conversation and was used to diminish the intensity of the psychic pain. Discovery of the process of this "secret" and his realizations that my interpretations were not attacks made it possible for him to "dose" himself with the active use of the virtual phantasy to control the intensity of his extreme anxiety. He could then inform me himself about these landing phantasies elaborated by full cockpit instrument readings bringing him home to the mother ship and immediately reducing his anxiety. Separation anxiety now occurred for the first time as he found the analytic sessions essential to his understanding of his work and family relations in which he noted similar feelings as had been previously described at the beginning of the session. At that time, he felt he needed the analysis more than the preservation of the learned virtual phantasy having discovered the effect of supervening numbness and loss of contact with both his family and work mates.

Describing the countertransference associated with my detection of a patient out of contact is challenging. The feeling of thinness which varies with one's approach is definitive. A verbal direct approach leads to an increased quality of "feeling of thinness." Excursions away from the point are usually relieving and can lead to a sense of enjoyment and safety. One often has the "sense" that one would be a lot wiser "not" to make a direct interpretation. Often there can be visually dominant language that can bring one's attention to a primary sensory mode being utilized. There can be an experience of being flooded by sensory communication. Close range or long range senses may be involved which can be used instrumentally to either distance or produce a lack of contact (Paul and Carson, 1980). If short range senses are used where long range experience would be appropriate, then one has touch, taste or smell rather than vision. In this mismatch a failure to connect is achieved. Virtual imagery in this regard is a good analogy as one has the impression of a false sense of focus when one looks at an object submerged in a pool of water. The apparent location is different than the actual location. In these individuals under description, their apparent location is different than their authentic location. This last point is a subjective impression, a general function of the countertransference and is inadequate for scientific purposes. One could raise the question, "Where is authentic location?" The response to be effective depends upon the analyst's capacity for at-one-ment with O (Bion, 1970).

I give this as a rather obvious use of a learned virtual phantasy to introduce the infinitude of forms which these phantasies can have. There can be forms of phantasy which are strictly virtual or others employing one or more internal sense derived images from memory which organize to produce a strong mental effect. This can involve the sense of security and especially reproducible "orientation" to the experience which is played in the mind to produce familiarity. I am concerned about whether or not there is a clear differentiation between what is being defined here as a virtual phantasy and the concept of internal unconscious phantasy as elaborated by Melanie Klein and Susan Isaacs (1970). What seems clear to me is that the organization by which these repeatable organized structures are transmitted to consciousness is in the service of suppression or inhibition of the emergence of a deeper, more primordial and ever more painful experience. These phantasies, in my experience, thus far dominate and organize the state of mind and lead to behaviors based on the conscious affects they induce. Their use seems to be organized as Column 2 elements (Bion, 1962) and prevent the flow of free association leading to discovery of deeper layers. The virtual fantasy that I described is stereotyped and is used as an inducer of replicable experience and is notable in that its usage becomes fixed. These fantasies are usually stimulating and produce strong images, sensations, and affects which give the sense-of being-in a situation which is grossly different than the circumstances of reality.

One striking example of the use of a virtual phantasy was notable in a sixty year old male engineer whose job entailed a highly technical liaison between the Air Force and various satellite communication encryption devices from ground to space and space to space organization of operations codes. This highly sophisticated, humorous, but very disturbed diminutive man, utilized imagery to convince himself that he was a teenaged girl which required a conscious feat of imagination. His visual fantasies involved transvestism of a stereotyped teenaged quality which had to change with the style. This fantasied disguise, which required secrecy, was a relief in the sense that it provided a feeling of safety and comfort and was a fixed world of phantasy, the primary organizer of which was fixed time so as to prevent getting older. The teenage girl fantasies were organized to be the opposite of being a sixty year old man concerned about aging and retirement. One quality of these phantasies is their involvement with sanctuary and control of the difficulties encountered by living in the real world—the trick is not to, while giving the illusion that one is. The "real" life is behind the scenes in the "simulator," however it is organized. In an earlier article, I described this man's concern with maintaining exact to the degree temperature regulation against drafts and air conditioning variations by wearing two to three pairs of long winter underwear (Paul, 1981). He could detect a single degree variation which produced severe anxiety and had a relation to a phantasy of being in the womb. Like a series of Chinese boxes, the teenage girl fantasy had to be analyzed before the more rigid and structured prenatal phantasies were elucidated and described. While some virtual fantasies are conscious and visual, they are often part of a deeper unconscious phantasy such as the above description.

The quality of time arresting constancy, sanctuary, and even pleasure, and a notable lack of persecutory experience is linked with a concrete rigidity and diminished use of projective identification. It is as though these individuals have been hermetically sealed and only are moved to pain when this autistic barrier is pierced. I want to emphasize the seeming normalcy of these individuals who appear "just like" others, talk "just like" others, and move "just like" whomever they imitate, "just like" or mimetic activity being the chief skill necessary to produce an effective disguise. These qualities are at least in part what I am using to differentiate these phantasies from those described by Klein and Isaacs. Often these "virtual fantasies" are preconscious. Even so, I would not like to claim them as being definitively different, but nonetheless worthy of description in their inductive role.

IV

The "control" of state of mind is inordinately complex. So far I have stressed the importance of voluntary processes directed by the individual. In addition, unconscious mental operations which can be seen to be quite elaborate may have a concrete quality similar to and/or leading to action. The example given below can be assigned a grid category, C6, (Bion, 1962) in which visual elements in a "dream" are ordered in a sequence which has a causal assumption. In previous months prior to this dream, the patient, a

45-year-old man who had been clearly psychotic and was in his tenth year of psychoanalysis, had allowed a separation from his elderly psychotic parents. He had been addicted to caring for them, in substitution for leading his own life. They could be counted upon to produce powerful, disturbing influences with astonishing regularity. Suffice to say that after exposure to either of them, he noted a severe diminution in his capacity to think and was so depressed, the psychic pain being so severe, that he took to bed, often recovering within several days. He timed these "exposures" so that the "threat" of effective external living, such as productive writing or involvement with a woman who was appropriate, could always be thwarted. In these activities, he used his parents' predictable stereotyped responses as an effective part of what could be thought of as a complex machine (Rube Goldberg) which had a defined, causal sequence. This negative response could effectively remove him from the field of external activity and maintain a time-arresting state of mind similar to his childhood during which painful sensations were created and maintained as an addiction. This orientation to an encapsulated time zone of feelings was constantly organized and reorganized in the transference.

A combination of steady work demonstrating the failure to actually arrest time showed him the delusional purpose of these activities. The thinning of the "capsule" allowed contact of a direct nature which was not only disorienting and extremely painful but allowed for work to go on in his creative writing that had a different character leading to development. Direct contact in which an interpretation was felt to penetrate showed, in that he remembered it and was able to compare the exact wording to recognize alterations he produced which previously would have slanted the meaning to harshness. This altered meaning would have been attributed to the analyst. After some years experience he was able to differentiate the distortions and "use" the interpretations to good account. This process had the unpleasant effect of demonstrating a kind of progress in the work that showed a time line in which it was clear that a gradation of ability to use the psychoanalytic work increased with years and was related to a diminution of delusional, paranoid activity. This recognition of time usually instituted a violent attack on linking, which would re-establish the sensuous, depressing affects he would produce by the establishment of a visual process, clearly leaving me out, and which was reported from his "capsule" at times in a manner that sounded as though the patient was enclosed in a large jar. In this "capsular phantasy," there could be an order reinstituted which led to sensation and not meaning, usually quite painful and communicated to me in such an intense way that it was very difficult for me to maintain contact. Sensations of numbness, deadness, and often intense depression, and a feeling that I can only describe as ploughing through a thick pudding, would occur with regularity upon any registration of time by the patient. We both became familiar with these phenomena, and he began gradually and now more urgently to be concerned about the "waste of time" and the "years going by" that could not be recouped no matter how precisely he could create and recreate the same affective states.

During this latter period of progress in the analysis, he related a dream, which he had taken to writing in a detailed notebook, and reported during periods of desperation. When he "gave up" the visual fantasizing encapsulated drugged state which he could recognize as a "mental masturbation" of a kind we had often detailed and would allow a "dosed" experience of contact in which he had the partial experience of "control," he felt anxious. Again, "control" meant that he had his mental foot on the brakes and felt that he could abate the terrifying feeling of disorientation which was no longer as overwhelmingly painful as before

A. He began, "If it isn't an action, what is it?" He then reported a dream. *I am looking at loading docks in my father's warehouse— these are long and narrow and not connected to the building. I am looking at a layer of concrete that needs to match some internal level—I see construction bolts—there is something there which needs to find a certain level to fit or something.*

B. *NASA has invented a device that blows an astronaut out of a building into a chute under air pressure leading into a cockpit. The chute does not connect—I'm worried about air turbulence flow—if the cockpit was closed it would create back pressure, so I tell my brother where the air is going (a) it came out of vents; (b) it recirculated through the engine—then I explained it to my brother. Once it's invented, now what? They don't need to invent anything else because that's how it's done from then on. They just keep repeating it. In this situation, it's where the answer is actually the death of the question.*

Then I'm seeing it from a big distance, as though I'm looking at slides—I'm seeing an image of the space shuttle—I'm bored with the images. There is a red one one with writing on it. A crowd is cheering on O.J. Simpson. The guys there must have been around a lot—he was charming, so they liked him. That's why they wrote what they wrote."

I interpreted that he was showing me a concrete communication in which, if he could raise the level of feeling, he could be blown out of his concrete bunker into an open cockpit that he was having engineering difficulties with. He could recognize the repetition and increasing distance from contact and instead of being fascinated with his virtuosity of image production, he was bored with it since he could realize the increasing distance from contact, no matter how elaborate his visual production was, the result was still the same, distance. The patient agreed, although I wasn't positive, that his response registered true agreement, but continued with the dream, which I hadn't realized I had interrupted.

I'm in a car, driving away with my girl. She leans over close to the guy next to her. I'm trying not to be jealous, like I shouldn't be. She's leaning over to be cuddly with another guy, and she's leaning back to be caught. Am I the kind of guy that would feel that way? Now I'm with my brother. I go to climb in bed and my mother's soiled diaper and bugs are there. My brother says there are gnats only and you can't sleep against plastic. I finish that conversation and I say is there something you want? I say this to mother. And she takes it very badly. I try to get her to want something.

My interpretation centered around his producing his own feelings, that is generating jealousy within himself to create distance rather than have contact with me and depending in specific upon the analytic work. He further produces a chain of causality by manufacturing feelings which have a palpable effect. He agreed to this and stated that that is what he means by "working things out for himself" and "getting my way." In terms of the issue of causality, I further detailed that the connection between his means of being able to establish a visual image or other sensory phantasy would produce a feeling as though his phantasy could lead to feeling in a direct causal form This process then produces an eventual sequence of phantasies and feelings. He could then feel that the contiguity of these mental events had a direct causal relation, one to the other, which then led to a quality of so-called "understanding," that further kept him in a capsular system in which he made the rules. The capsular system is represented by the cockpit in which he can no longer be perfectly enclosed in without severe "engineering difficulties." I continued, "Not only does he make the rules in this particular system, but that the words and the language that is utilized to speak to the outside world, in this instance myself, 'seems' to be articulate speech but in fact is an imitation of it organized for the purpose of generating a particular set of phantasies and feelings but also meant to keep a barrier between himself and myself."

A dream several weeks later further revealed a further stage of the presentation of imitative speech in a much less concrete way as many of the issues had achieved symbolic representation through the analytic work.

A. *A youth is lean and bare-chested, worried about getting sunburned. I tell him we do not have to stay long after the sun comes up, one does not have to stay that long, and we'll do our work while we're there.*

B. *There is a three foot wall in the shape of an L. On either side of the wall, there is a game between single guys and single girls. A game show host is calling out the name Allan, and lots of guys respond to the name. Is it "cool" to lie? There can't be all that many Allans. I'm nervous about getting ready for when I get called on. I'm exposed and want to put on some underpants, so I see boxer shorts that have a hole in them, and I put them on over my shorts. They look okay. The guy that was being called on is asked his age. I don't want to tell. I would try to avoid making it an issue. I couldn't be natural about it.*

C. *The host starts to demonstrate what the guy had been called on to do. He is acting some part. Instantly, he's got tears. Then he's able to put on a laugh—I'm really surprised he's doing it. He's getting a lot of practice acting and I'm impressed. I say I'd hire him as an actor. There is a guy in front of me who is related to the host. I ask if it's his brother? He says it's his father. These guys look ethnic (Middle Eastern). He knows Yiddish and all sorts of Jewish stuff but he's not Jewish. He's learned all that stuff.*

D. *My friend B asks him what time Kaddish is? We'll do our version of it at the beach. This guy is dressed bizarrely, (the host). Layers of leotards, too small, not pulled up all the way like he's a fool. My mother would get stuck with her pants pulled down. Not on all the way.*

E. *Next I'm walking with my girlfriend who is very young and pretty and it's nice. We're young. There is a crowd of others and it's new. But I see "R," an old friend from high school. She is an experimental psychologist at Yale now and just got, separated from Allan (in actuality). Suddenly I'd forgotten my girlfriend's name—I turn away to stall for time. I ask him questions about what her name is. I don't like that name. It begins with an "M". Melissa... Margaret... I go through the alphabet to see if that triggers something. A saleslady overhears the noises I am making and she thinks that there is something wrong. I say I'm just putting vowels and consonants together, trying to remember something. Trying to come up with the girl's name.* (Here in my own countertransference experience I think remember-dismember.)

F. *I massage the saleslady's back—she shows me some jewelry and tries to explain to me that my mom is making it hard for herself... to make selections about which jewels. My mother thinks she needs to look up the individual components... all the beads in the catalogue in order to make a selection. If she were the manufacturer, that's what she'd have to do. Mom shows up with this piece looking like curly lettuce or a sea plant which is white... what they had on display wasn't white, it was clear transparent, so she found what she liked... I admire that and it seems like a waste but if she doesn't buy things often, she's entitled to it. I'd come up with the idea to ask the store to hold it. Maybe it will talk her out of it but maybe it won't be lost. It cost a thousand dollars, but if it's given to my sister, she'll lose it in her junk or break it. She couldn't tell the difference between junk and valuable stuff and I can't tell the difference either.*

I am reporting a paraphrasing of interpretations of the dream interspersed with the dream text.

a. The confusion about work is represented. He feels he is being exposed to radiation which he is afraid will burn him (the analysis). He is told that the time, is short (that is life) and his exposure is limited, that is he can control the exposure, and that time is emerging as having meaning. The time of his life, suddenly relates to the time in a session. The limits of time being short as a model for the changing experience of life from infinite time to limited and particular time.

b. In the B section, there is a reference to the use of language in meeting women. (There has always been a terror of this and an "act" has been maintained.) Should he lie? He always has, and now it's just coming through to him, as he has always dated women 20 years or so younger and has been frustrated. He has been confused about this since he "looks" much younger and has been able to "act" in a such a way so that younger women think he is "cool," and timely (current style) to them (precisely how his father behaves at the age of 86) but he is afraid that the analytic process is catching him with his pants down so that he feels humiliated as a result of the discovery of his ruse to himself or the lie which produces embarrassment (bare ass) upon discovery. Boxer shorts are a reference to his martial arts stance in the transference and in life and feeling of a general fear that he will be discovered as a phony or an imitation.

c. The analytic process reveals to him his increasing awareness of his fabrication of reality to someone else (being someone or acting like someone he is not), an actor, and his continued confusion about his skill and use of acting. He gets lost in time while his friend, B, asks him what time Kaddish is, which is an appropriate use of a ritual but nonetheless an effective reference to death (an end to fabrication and a clear reference to facts). There are clear references to, his mother caught with her pants down, soiling, which she actually does, and the host father who acts big and dresses bizarrely—a fool—who also denies who he is and his age.

d. The wish to be young and happy with a nice, normal girlfriend is intruded upon by time again. The woman R, who represents a friend of 30 years ago in high school in actuality, is seen and shows up— suddenly he changes his state of mind and gets confused. He forgets the young girl's name and tries to fabricate it out of sounds, vowels, and consonants, going through the alphabet to see if it triggers something. He recognizes that for him speech is making infantile sounds without meaning. The saleslady, discovering something wrong, represents the part of him referencing communication to the outside as disordered and an imitation of human speech. "I'm just going through the vowels and consonants to remember the girl's name." These references clearly demonstrate an increasing awareness by the more developed part of himself identified with the analyst of problems that have reached enough significance to himself to be symbolized and apperceived.

e. Mother thinking that she needs to "look up all the original compo- nents, all the beads in the catalogue" illustrates a difficulty in trusting words as though one could better understand if all the letters or individual components could be compared in the "catalog-alphabet" in order to get them across as meaning (make or sell them). Language has been so defaced that there is the sense that it has to be invented anew. What can be added as creativity is doubted, as "creativity" cannot be distinguished from meaningless distortion.

f. There is an aspect of him identified with his mother who puts ideas together in an interesting way but is unable to use them as currency because their representation, although creative, is idio-syncratic and not suitable for use in communication as words are, which accurately stand for something. Until now, these creations have been lost, but now they are close enough to be recognized as jewels which may have a use, not merely for decoration. They are valuable. Much of the communication actually spoken to his sister is misused or treated as junk and cannot be developed. If he could better differentiate between value and mental detritus, he could decide what to use and what is not valuable for communication. These are references to the products of his mind which represent the alpha elements suitable for use in symbol formation which can lead to unique jewels demonstrating his creativity if they were not mixed with other defaced and blunted aspects of mental process which make them indistinguishable from rubbish. He hopes that there can be a containment long enough to differentiate them through the analytic process and that he can store them so that they can be retrieved and differentiated. The sea plant looking like curly lettuce is not the same as that which they have on display (common use) for that is a reference to invention and it is also reference to the opacity of his use of language; that is, it is not clear like the one on display.

The problems with which the patient must deal involve fundamental difficulties in the formal operations of thinking. He must avoid contact to remain "encapsulated" yet the lysis of the barrier reveals to him increasing difficulties about verbal thought and communication. He faces the severe humiliation that he has "imitated human speech" making noises which, rather than communicating a precise symbolic meaning to himself and then to someone else, various substitutes occur. He has used verbal thought to induce visual phantasies which give him the image he wishes to believe and has remained deluded even throughout the analytic process which has demonstrated these delusions and hallucinations to him. He has realized that he believed he had to maintain these images to allay fears of cata-strophic change and intensely painful affect which he could not tolerate. His use of "reversible perspective" (Bion, 1962) having been discovered by both of us hindered his use of it, yet evasion had to be maintained in order to avert catastrophe. Increasing awareness of his associations being evasions and lies led to intense pain, yet could only be given up in slow increments as his pain tolerance increased. The recognition of his use of imitative noises sounding like human speech has been grievously upsetting. His subsequent inability to value the analyst's communications because they utilize articu-late speech which has never been trusted is a consequence. Vowels and consonants produce sounds which have an action, trigger memories, induce affects and images but have not been organized to stand for something and could not be confidently used to represent meaning. This has led the patient to despair relating to his use of both conscious and unconscious insincerity. Severe difficulties with memory and the maintenance of continuity of thought are evident. These problems directly relate to the inability to "store" received verbal communication complicated by deflection of attention and degraded alpha elements only suitable for evacuation.

References to having to derive meaning from letters and the basic syllables of words are referred to in the dream material (mother thinking she needs to look up the individual components—all the beads in the catalogue to make a selection as though she were the manufacturer). Going through the alphabet to see if it triggers something demonstrates the kind of maneuver one sees in a Korsakoff's psychosis in which fabrications are utilized craftily to hide the fact that there is a gap in memory or blank in consciousness. The saleslady, overhearing his "noises," is an indicator that he is increasingly aware of his "putting vowels and consonants together" in a different way (again an imitation of speech). The saleslady represents an aspect of his personality organized to sell his language-act to the outer world, and when she acknowledges the apperceived difficulty, he massages her to seduce her (message/ massage), a primitive pun.

The references to the ethnic types who learned "all that Jewish stuff" involves contempt for those who mouth phrases and sounds in a language for which they have no understanding of the symbolic verbal content but pass off their use of sounds as though it were understanding. One can see the split attitude toward lying and the conscious "con job," that is the confidence game attitude which is felt to be far superior to the truth.

References to bringing together defaced elements of mother and father in verbal form involve a destructive, hateful version of the primal scene contributing to both the concretism and disordered creativity which plays a role in his mistrust of language.

V

I want to paraphrase and quote from W.R. Bion's (1955) "Language and the Schizophrenic." Bion referred to Freud's 1924 paper on "Neurosis and Psychosis" in which an, important distinction between these categories is made. "Neurosis is the result of a conflict between the ego and its id, whereas psychosis is the analogous outcome of a similar disturbance in the relation to the ego and its environment (outer world)" (p. 220). Bion reminds us that Freud's formula points to the psychotic patient's hostility to reality, and conflict with it, which enables us to grasp one element that determines the nature of endopsychic conflict.

In reference to Freud's 1911 article, "Formulations Regarding the Two Principles of Mental Functioning," Bion quotes,

> The increasing significance of external reality heightened the significance also of the sense organs directed toward that outer world, and of the consciousness attached to them; the latter now learned to comprehend the qualities of sense in addition to the qualities of pleasure and "pain" which hitherto had alone been of interest to it (p. 221).

It will be one of my contentions that the conflict with reality leads the psychotic patient to developments which make it doubtful whether he has ever learned to "comprehend the qualities of sense in addition to the qualities of pleasure and pain." Further, I shall suggest there is evidence which may indicate that destructive attacks have been directed by the patient, or the patient's id, against the newly significant sense organs and "the consciousness attached to them" (p. 221).

In my view, what Freud describes as the institution of the reality principle is an event that has never been satisfactorily achieved by the psychotic, and the main failure takes place at the point which Melanie Klein describes as the development of the depressive position. The reality principle, if it were allowed to operate, would make the psychotic infant aware of his relationship with whole objects, and thereby of the feelings of depression and guilt associated with the depressive position. It is at this point, however, that the patient makes destructive attacks on those aspects of his personality, his ego, that are concerned with establishing external contact and internal contact. What are these special aspects of the ego? Freud cites (1) attention; (2) notation, which he says is a part of that which we call memory; (3) an impartial passing of judgment; 4) a new function entrusted to motor discharge which is now concerned with action; and 5) restraint of action by means of a process of thought which was developed from ideation (p. 221).

Freud states:

Thought was endowed with qualities which made it possible for the mental apparatus to support increased tension during a delay in the process of discharge. It is essentially an experimental way of acting, accompanied by displacement of smaller quantities, of cathexis together with less expenditure (discharge of them) (p. 222).

Bion states that he thinks that all these special adaptations (except 4) are really aspects of the establishment of verbal thought; further, that this development is one aspect of the synthesizing and integrating forces which Melanie Klein has described as characteristic of the depressive position. Bion (1955) regards "disturbance in the development of verbal thought as an important aspect of psychosis, particularly, but not exclusively of schizophrenia" (p. 222). He continues,

Castration of the ego is identical with destructive attacks on (1) the consciousness attached to the sense organs; (2) attention—the function which Freud says is instituted to search the outer world; (3) the system of notation which he describes as part of memory; (4) the passing of judgment which was developed to take the place of repression; and finally (5) thought as a way of supporting the increased tension produced by the restraint on motor discharge. With regard to this last point, I would add that in my view, verbal thought is the essential feature of all five functions of the ego and that the destructive attacks on verbal thought or its rudiments is inevitably an attack on all (p. 222).

Bion makes clear that he believes that the same oral, urethral, anal, and muscular sadism that Melanie Klein (1930) describes as typical of the attacks on the mother's body is an action against the ego. The "castration" of the ego then is manifested in extremely sadistic attacks on all the aforementioned ego functions. Especially relevant is the capacity to support frustration of motor discharge which is dependent upon the development of verbal thought of which the above-enumerated functions are particular aspects. "The splitting of verbal thought is carried out cruelly, and the attempts at synthesis which are typical in psychotics, as in others, of the depressive position are frustrated because the splits are brought together cruelly" (p. 223). Bion brings to the paper a final point which is unfortunately often ignored, that the splitting mechanism is brought into action to minister to the patient's greed and is therefore not simply an unfortunate catastrophe of the kind that occurs when the patient's ego is split in pieces as an accompaniment of his determination to split his objects; "it is the outcome of a determination which can be expressed verbally as an intention to be as many people as possible so as to be in as many places as possible, so as to get as much as possible, for as long as possible—in fact timelessly" (p. 223).

What has this all to do with the imitation of human speech? In accurate verbal thought, words are utilized to refer to something which has a common currency, either something which is thought or which is perceived as part of the external world. Then, an imitation of human speech would sound "like" real speech that has certain essential differences. It could betray the attacks on the ego's capacity for attention, notation, judgment, restraint on motor action and thought, in a more subtle way than would be evident in schizophrenia but would be less violently noticeable Life in the encapsulated state for these individuals would follow in a less obvious way Freud's formula for psychosis since insulation from the outside world is the goal organized by the primordial conscience.

In "Notes on the Penitential Transference" (1989), I described the "danger" signals of "psychic movement" and demonstrated the derailing or deflecting attacks organized to put a stop to the awareness of change. The attacks on the perceptual organs which Bion (1955) described so profoundly aid in the maintenance of a phantasy of a timeless hermetic seal. In critical observation of patients in this state of mind, it is clear that there are severe distortions of judgment based on failure to accurately perceive and process incoming stimuli. Attention and notation are seriously compromised as well by the attacks on perception. While these points are quite clear in a severely compromised individual, detecting the "problem of imitation" becomes more difficult when the encapsulated state is not so obvious. In this less obvious state, the capacity for attention can be quite developed but for the purpose of maintaining a distance from true contact in which there is penetration of the mind coming from the other. That is, it must "seem" as though there is contact, especially verbally, and that there is an intellectual process in operation which "satisfies" the other member of the pair or group in conversation that there has been a receipt of the communication and a response which is apposite. "Success" of the mimetic communication can be judged by the perpetrator by the lack of penetration or confrontation coming from the other. It is clear when the responder in this case, the psychoanalyst, does not accept at face value the distancing, off point communication, and draws attention to the problem at hand. This operation may produce penetration to the point at which it becomes noticeable to the analysand and immediately ushers in a disturbing resistance, either a full stop or a kind of defensive explosion organized to reestablish the hermetic seal by distancing the analyst and the language of true effect. This can appear as a form of the negative therapeutic reaction in which the patient will typically miss sessions or even bolt the analysis. As can be seen, this kind of confrontative analytic work takes considerable skill and that the progress jerks in starts and stops, the patient moving away from contact. Robert Caper (1995) has referred to noticing in the countertransference an anxiety as to whether one should make the interpretation which can be foreseen by the analyst to lead to a disturbance. It is as if the patient has said, "Here's the line and don't you dare cross it or else!" This hostility is definitely a function of the psychic pain and disorientation produced by the penetrating interpretation.

Bion (1955) makes the point clear that the development of verbal thought is a function of the integrative processes described by Melanie Klein (1930) as the depressive position. There is the immediate pain brought on by the awareness of guilt and lost time as well as the anxiety relating to needing an object that can abandon one, linked to the awareness of having damaged that object. In Bion's example (1955), the recognition of insanity is brought about by the analytic process and specifically by the development of verbal thought that is felt by the patient to have led to the difficulties. The depressive position emerges and the hatred of recognition of his delusions and hallucinated mental life occurs. The analyst must be prepared for severe emotional storms at this point and "concentrate on not allowing the patient to retreat from his realization that he is insane or from his hatred of the analyst who has succeeded, after so many years, in bringing him to an emotional realization of the facts which he has spent his life trying to evade" (p. 235).

REFERENCES

Bion, W.R. (1955). Language and the schizophrenic. In: Klein, M., Heimann, P., Money-Kyrle, R. (Eds.), *New Directions in Psychoanalysis*. London: Tavistock Pubns., pp. 220-239.

—— (1962). *Learning from Experience*. London: Heinemann.

—— (1970). *Attention and Interpretation*. London: Tavistock Pubns.

Caper, R. (1995). On the difficulty of making a mutative interpretation. *Int. J Psycho-Anal.*, 76: 91-101

Freud, S. (1911). Formulations on the Two Principles of Mental Functioning, *S.E.*, 12, 1958, pp. 218-226. In: J. Strachey (Ed.), *The Standard Edition of the Complete Psychological Works of Sigmund Freud*. 24 volumes. London: The Hogarth Press and The Institute of Psycho-Analysis, 1953-1974.

Isaacs, S. (1970). The nature and function of phantasy. In: Klein, M., Heimann, P., Isaacs, S., Rivière, J. (Eds.), *Developments in Psychoanalysis*. London: Hogarth Press.

Klein, M. (1930), The Importance of Symbol-Formation in the Development of the Ego, in: Klein, M., *Love, Guilt and Reparation, and Other Works: 1921-1945*. New York: The Free Press, 1975, pp. 219-232.

Meltzer, D.W., Brenner, J., Hoxter, S., Weddell, H., Wittenberg, I. (1975). *Explorations in Autism*. Perthshire: Clunie Press.

Paul, M.I. (1981). A mental atlas of the process of psychological birth. In: J. S. Grotstein (Ed.), *Do I Dare Disturb the Universe? A Memorial to Wilfred R. Bion*. Beverly Hills: Caesura Press, pp. 552-570.

—— (1989). Notes on the primordial development of the penitential transference. *M. Klein Obj. Rel.*, 7(2): 43-69.

—— (1989). Intonational elements as communication in psychoanalysis. *Free Assns.*, 15: 67-86.

—— (1993). A consideration of practical psychoanalytic epistemology. *M. Klein Obj. Rel.*, 11(2): 11-29.

Paul, M.I., Carson, I.M. (1980). A contribution to the study of dimension. *Int. Rev. Psycho-Anal.*, 7: 101-111.

Tustin, F. (1981). Psychological birth and psychological catastrophe. In: Tustin, F., *Autistic States in Children*. London: Routledge, pp. 78-94.

20038 Pacific Coast Hway
Malibu CA 90265
USA

JOURNAL OF MELANIE KLEIN AND OBJECT RELATIONS
Vol. 15, No. 1, March 1997

DOES MIND HAVE BOUNDARIES
IN THE WAY THAT BODY DOES?

Eric Rhode

The other day, as I had a first session with a new patient, I became aware
of how I was clinging to his speech, as though moving by touch along a
surface. I was conscious of the way in which his sentences were constructed.
They were put together like bits of mosaic. The joins between the mosaic bits
might have been gaps, blurs, disappearances of themes, and half themes.
Esther Bick (1968) and Donald Meltzer *et al.* (1975) have described a type of
identification that they have called adhesive. My contact with this mosaic
surface was adhesive.

At the same time, I recollected another type of response to a patient.
Obviously there are many ways of responding to a patient but these two
responses came together. I recollected how W.R. Bion had said that it was
important to put up with the experience of a session and to observe the facts
in a state of not knowing until a pattern began to emerge. This is not clinging
to a surface, this is letting yourself go into deep space, the "not knowing" of
a session; sometimes, as though you were at one with a dying or dismem-
bered being.

Later I thought—as I often had thought before—how important and how
strange Bion's formulation was. After all, he does not say you observe and
observe until you *see* a pattern, which makes sense in a cause and effect way.
He says: put up with something, and observe the thing you put up with,
and then with luck and in time, and perhaps as a *non sequitur*, you may be
aware of an emerging pattern. But a pattern that emerges from where?

Bion came to his view of how one should work by way of a crisis in
confidence. The crisis brought about changes in his way of thinking. I shall
illustrate this change with a fragment of clinical material. Over the years the
meaning of this fragment underwent a change in Bion's mind, or so I infer
from the evidence I am going to present. I do not know whether Bion
himself was aware of this particular process of transformation.

Bion (1979) describes the crisis in *The Dawn of Oblivion*, which is the third
book in his novel *A Memoir of the Future*—or rather Bion has a character

called "Psycho-Analyst" who describes a crisis that sounds not unlike Bion's own experiences.

The character called "Psycho-Analyst" says:

> I found it difficult to understand Klein's theory and practice though—perhaps because—I was being analyzed by Melanie Klein herself. But after great difficulty I began to feel that there was truth in the interpretations and that they brought illumination to many experiences, mine and others, which had previously been incomprehensible, discrete and unrelated. Metaphorically, light began to dawn and then, with increasing momentum, all was clear... One of the painful, alarming features of continued experience was the fact that I had certain patients with whom I employed interpretations based on my previous experience with Melanie Klein, and though I felt that I employed them correctly and could not fault myself, none of the good results that I anticipated occurred (1979, pp. 121-122).

The chance reading of three texts had him persist in his work. Let me list these texts quite summarily.

1. He re-read Freud's obituary of Charcot, in which Freud stated that he had been impressed by "Charcot's insistence on continued observation of facts— unexplained facts—until a pattern emerged."

2. Elsewhere in Freud, he once more read Freud's "admission that the 'trauma of birth' might afford a plausible but misleading reason for believing that there was a caesura [i.e. gap] between natal and pre-natal. There were other impressive 'caesuras'—for example between conscious and unconscious—which might be similarly misleading" (p. 122).

3. He re-read John Milton's evocation to light at the beginning to the Third Book of *Paradise Lost*. "I re-read the whole of *Paradise Lost* in a way which I had not previously done, although I had always been devoted to Milton. This was likewise true of Virgil's *Aeneid*" (p. 122).

A quotation from Milton gives the essence of what Bion calls the religious vertex. "The rising world of waters dark and deep [are] won from the void and formless infinite" (cf. 1965, p. 151).

The literary critic William Empson (1961) has written that Milton's *Paradise Lost* put him in the mind of the brutal and splendid west African sculpture of Benin. "I think it horrible and wonderful; I regard it as like Aztec or Benin sculpture, or to come nearer home the novels of Kafka, and

I am rather suspicious of any critic who claims not to feel anything so obvious" (p. 13).

How is it possible to move from Freud's conception of mind and thought as arising out of the biological processes of body—as in his famous dictum that the ego is body ego—to the truly barbaric and patriarchal suppositions of Milton's *Paradise Lost*, in which it is claimed that the material as well as the ideal universe arises out of a void?

We put up with the void or silence out of which the session arises, as though faced by first creation. This might be evidence of a primitive civilization, a primitive catastrophe, or perhaps both.

Bion indicates that in every session there are at least two vertices, or points of view, of a global nature. The two vertices that concern him are the medical and the religious vertices. Both are essential to the creating of the dimension in which psychoanalytic thinking occurs. *Transference will founder if the couple in therapy damage or degrade one or other of the vertices.* If you can experience the two vertices in the room, you may experience them as creating the imaginative space out of which the thinking of psychoanalysis arises.

Both the vertices operate in the same way: they unfold like a chain. They resemble the ancient world's view of the cosmos as a great chain of being, as in Arthur Lovejoy's (1936) description of it. They start at some certain point and move out to the edge of intuition—what the ancients thought of as the end of the world. In their chaining they are a rudimentary form of rationalism, although it may be more accurate to say that in their structure they are like music.

The medical vertex begins from an idealized conception of the body as a whole entity. (Actually, it begins as a way of coping with the crisis of epidemic.) Body discloses itself as male and female versions of itself. The religious vertex begins from the void; and the void emanates two types of hallucination. One type of hallucination represents being, the other type represents non being. Both vertices carry within them an. Bion thinks of it as the contact barrier. It contains zero function. Zero function is auto destruct: definitions destroy themselves as they form.

In the religious vertex "gaps," which is what I want now to focus on, have a different meaning from "gaps" in the medical vertex. They can be indications of the becoming of "O", a mode of internalization that cannot be known and only inferred as a variable.

In the medical vertex there is an idealization of continuity. The concept of duration is viewed as fundamental to the notion of "experience." There is trust, to the point of credulity, in the postulate that the fact of succession in space and time is a basis for truth. Discontinuity tends to be related to the meaningless, even to the destruction of meaning. In the religious vertex, on the other hand, discontinuity may be a source for meaning.

I now want to look at some clinical material taken from Bion's writings concerning discontinuity and to show how his views on discontinuity changed over the years. Starting from the medical vertex, Bion describes discontinuity in terms of psychotic "gaps." With the passing of time, his concept of gap changes from a medical to a religious vertex reading—by way of a particular incident. Over the years his imagination was able to transform remarkably the meaning that a certain patient conveyed to him concerning some holes in a pair of socks.

At the Eighteenth International Psycho-Analytic Congress in 1953, Bion gave a paper called "Notes on the Theory of Schizophrenia". In his paper Bion referred to a patient who said to him. "I pick a tiny piece of skin from my face and feel quite empty." Later the patient said, "I do not feel able to buy any new clothes and my socks are a mass of holes" (in 1967, p. 28). Whether intentionally or not, the patient made a link between the idea of skin with holes in it and the knitting together of holes that may result in a pair of socks.

At the time the patient made these remarks, Bion was put in mind of one of Freud's papers, *The Unconscious* (*SE 14*, p. 198 ff.). In *The Unconscious* Freud writes about a patient who presented similar worries concerning skin holes and other forms of skin disturbance. Freud refers to papers by two of his colleagues, whose patients had been preoccupied by holes in skins and socks.

When Bion first heard his patient make the (perhaps) unconscious link between skin holes and sock holes, he was inclined to take up the link—as Freud once had done—from within the medical vertex. Now the medical vertex operates from some notion of continuity, tactile skin continuity, if you like. It is opposed to knowledge derived from the void. It assumes that if there is a gap in knowledge this gap can be filled because somewhere there is a dictionary, call it history possibly, which can fill any gap.

Implicit in the medical vertex is the belief that everything can be answered. It conceives of experience as primarily an embodiment. It has no place in it for a concept of unknowable internalization—a concept of unknowable becoming. It quantifies life as an idealized span of time that everyone has a right to. It sees tactile continuity is a form of legitimized boundary. Skin holes and sock holes are signs, whose meanings lie in some master dictionary which is to hand—in the form of various types of classification: some being derived from psychiatry, from medical lore itself; others, like the theory of the complexes, being derived from Greek literature or from Greek idealism.

Working within this vertex, Bion thought that his patient had made a hypochondriac or phobic assertion and had given voice to unconscious phantasies concerning the sensation of somebody's body, perhaps even his own body, body being a form of universal grammar. He thought to "explain" the patient's experiences by referring to the psychiatric literature, as though it were an equivalent to Fowler's *Dictionary of Modern English Usage*.

But then Bion came into contact, or rather failed to make contact, with a patient to whom this approach made no sense. Bion found that none of his uses of previously tested theory had any effect in helping him make contact with the patient.

In the meanwhile, the patient had begin to find (in a comparable failure of reference) that his ability to use language in the sessions had lost any meaning. He spoke in disjointed clauses, then single words, then stopped speaking. Body and language and the language of the body seized up. Both men were reduced to giving up any pre-established notion of continuity. They had to put up with each other and to endure silence.

And of course the silence was a version of the skin and sock type of gap. A sophisticated person might have said that the gap represented the discontinuity implicit in the concept of continuity. Or that the gap represented the inconceivable, a truly metaphysical concept. But this is to leap ahead.

You have to wait and put up with considerable discomfort if you wish for the inconceivable to speak to you. In such a context, of waiting for the inconceivable to speak to you, the body-centered thinking of the medical vertex loses some of its power. The classifications of anatomy are important: it is one among two possibilities that the experience indicates. The other possibility is of body used as a sign language for other powers.

In later years Bion believed that the only person he could learn from was his patient, even though the patient might present himself as a void or gap or a text full of blanks. Theories concerning other patients could only get in the way. Bion thought that it was evidence of tiredness in a session if he got a rush of theories to the head. He had to put up with the facts until the pattern emerged.

Bion's crisis began to modify when he recognized that certain patients were using projection in their sessions not to intrude or to destroy somebody or something, but as a means of preverbal communication, sometimes of a pain that they could not tolerate; or that they were entering into states of hallucinatory modulation between the senses in a way that put Bion in mind of mathematical computation—that is, of a high cultural achievement.

Fourteen years after his initial public reading of "otes on the Theory of Schizophrenia," Bion republished the paper in 1967, in a collection of papers called *Second Thoughts*. His outlook had changed. Adding a commentary to the paper, he asserted that there was "no satisfactory psycho-analytic model" for the experiences of his "On Arrogance" patient. He felt that his patient's "... 'mental boundary' had lost an important part of itself through his destructive attack on it. He was now attacked by the 'hole' which was part of his mental skin... a residual after he had wrought his destruction" (p. 142).

Bion gives a dramatic or mythic description to psychic talion. You attack your skin, as though it were the skin to someone's mind, and the damaged object then attacks you. Bion asserts that in order to extend "psycho-analytic theory to cover the view of mystics from the *Bhagavad Gita* to the present," he wishes to claim that his patient had "an attitude to the persecuting holes which ultimately showed features [that] we find in a religious attitude to idols" (p. 145).

In terms of concrete thinking, gaps are idols—and idols are gaps. Some people seek to personify and name the gap, perhaps as a nameless dread. The continuum, and any conceivable break in it, begin to separate: the continuum transforms into the immanence of the natural world, while the break in the continuum gives utterance to a transcendental and supernatural order.

In *Paradise Lost* John Milton asserts that you can only apprehend psychic reality by first forfeiting sensation, that is bodily knowledge. As a ritual instance of this knowing of the gap, John Milton refers to the need for actual or symbolic blindness as a prerequisite for psychic knowledge. Are blind visionaries of the kind that Milton describes similar to foetuses in whose optic pits eyes have not yet formed? This is a medical-vertex question that fascinated Bion in his later years. At the same time he asks the religious vertex version of this question: Is Miltonic "blindness" the means by which the gap transforms into the contact barrier?

In Bion's thought the gap has now become the void, the formless infinite, something that he describes as the nameless "O". Milton's "rising world of waters dark and deep [are] won from the void and formless infinite" (cf. 1965, p. 151).

It is helpful to link the John Milton quotation to the two themes taken from Bion's reading of Freud: the need to tolerate the facts of a situation until a pattern emerges, and the belief in an implicit integrity between pre-natal and post-natal types of knowledge.

In the religious vertex, mind operates by yoking together dissimilarities often in ways that bring out their incongruity, as in the violent yoking together of heterogeneous ideas in seventeenth-century "metaphysical" poetry.[1] Milton's theory yokes together dissimilarities in a manner that someone concerned with the importance of tactile continuity may find incomprehensible.

If science is concerned with the relationships of similarities, as in the relationship of grain and bread, which entails a knowledge of subtle and sometimes inaccessible processes related to biology, agriculture and cooking, then religious thought is concerned with radical dissimilarities, like the relationship of an incarnated and murdered god to a piece of bread, or the relationship between Mosaic stone-tables, on which are carved a cosmic blueprint, and a void out of which the stone-tables emerged.

The forms that are wrested from "the void and the formless infinite" do not differ from the embodied world of the medical world in terms of degree; they differ in kind. And there is no dictionary, or corpus of established definitions, by which they can be squared with one another.

Any break in continuity of touch is disturbing enough; but the state of disturbance is increased by the fact that the discontinuity gives rise to a type of experience that continuity has not prepared it for: a primordial experience in which we know gaps as idols rather than as absences. Bion show his readers that these idols might be icons: that they incarnate something, rather than act as delusional defenses against nothing. The principle of sufficient reason *can* apply to hallucination.

Certain countertransference responses need time; they may come to mind long after a therapeutic relationship has ended. Seven years after the publication of "Notes on the Theory of Schizophrenia" in his book *Second Thoughts*—exactly twenty years after the first reading of the paper in public —Bion returned to the experience of the socks with holes in them in his *Brazilian Lectures*, and he gave it an interpretation which owes as much to Milton as to Freud's posthumous appreciation of Charcot. He says:

> We might look at a pair of socks and be able to see a mass of holes which have been knitted together. Freud... said that the patient had a phobia which made it impossible for him to wear socks. I suggest that the patient did not have a phobia of socks but could see that what Freud thought were socks were a lot of holes knitted together (1973, in 1990, p. 21).

Bion then imagines "... a penetrating beam of darkness [which is] a reciprocal of the searchlight." (This is a version of John Milton's act of self-blinding.) He continues:

> The peculiarity of this penetrating ray is that it could be directed towards the object of our curiosity, and this object would absorb whatever light already existed, leaving the area of examination exhausted of any light that it possessed. The darkness would be so absolute that it would achieve a luminous, absolute vacuum. So that, if any object existed, however faint, it would show up very clearly. Thus, a faint light would become visible in maximum conditions of darkness...
>
> ... Suppose we are watching a game of tennis, looking at it with increasing

darkness. We dim the intellectual illumination and light, forgetting imagination or phantasy or any once-conscious activities: first we lose sight of the players, and then we gradually increase the darkness until only the net itself is visible. If we can do this, it is possible to see that the only important thing visible to us is a lot of holes which are collected together in a net (1973, in 1990, pp. 20-21).

Losing contact with the world by way of sight, losing the ability to use eyes as though they were a way of touching or being touched, arouses a premonition filled with dread. How can it be related to visionary truth? The premonition is one of having to meet the psychotic element in ourselves (or others) without the intermediary of the contact barrier; or it may be concerned with acts of mutilation, again of oneself or of someone other. Or it may be concerned with the act of falling asleep and of losing the world of sense knowledge and possibly discovering the world of dreams.

The couple who play tennis, the primal couple perhaps, disappears; or rather an image disappears, as its underlying meaning comes to the fore, a glowing reticulation, an indication of thought's concealed syntax that the non psychotic parts of the mind do not see, a primal articulation that spills out of mind into the universe as a cosmology. In awe we release primal articulation into the significance and beauty of the night sky filled with stars.

In terms of the medical vertex, the reticulation is an idol: a delusion that insulates thought from a dread of the void. In the medical vertex, hallucination is idolic. In terms of the religious vertex, the reticulation is an icon. It arises on the boundary between life and death. It is agent for the experience of the gap in the transference. I know the reticulation most familiarly in daily life in my pleasure in music. I said to a musician who inclines to psychosis, "music arises on the boundary between life and death" and he answered—"of course."

The reticulation is the contact barrier: a means of making contact, or of touching, the inconceivable. In *Dawn of Oblivion* Bion writes, "It was as if, literally as well as metaphorically, light began to grow, night was replaced by dawn" (p. 122).

The world that I know spatially may not be the world as it is, because erroneously I derive phantasies of the world from my senses used as touch. Even the sight of a glowing reticulation is not secure. Bion recalls that mankind for generations misguidedly believed that Euclidean space was the only type of space to exist. But the fact that sensation is used to realize a certain kind of space does not entail that it is the only type of space that might exist.

Bion refers

to the extreme capacity for observation which is natural to some patients. Just as it is natural for me in my gross, macroscopic way classically to see a pair of socks, this kind of patient has a visual capacity which is different, making him able to see what I cannot see... We must be able to see that it is a pair of socks, or a game of tennis, and at the same time be able to turn down the light, turn off the brilliant intuition, and see these holes, including the fact that they are knitted, or netted together... I would like to consider the category "psychotic" and suggest that it is too gross, too macroscopic. If we look at it more closely, in detail, in the way we would have to look at a game of tennis, or a pair of socks, we can see that there may be *insane* psychotics and *sane* psychotics. It might be possible to help the insane psychotic to become an efficient psychotic (1973, in 1990, p. 21).

He adds: "It depends on a certain flexibility of mind in all of us who concern ourselves with the human mind" (p. 22).

The theme of reticulation is implicit in the "On Arrogance" paper. At the time when patient and therapist were most unable to be in touch with the other, Bion recollected the figure of the sphinx in the play of *Oedipus*. The sphinx is an other-worldly being who destroys stability in the human mind by the riddles it asks. As a persecuted representation of the contact barrier between patient and therapist (contact barrier collapsed into beta screen), the sphinx becomes the interface between them both and shows a different aspect of itself to each of them. "It is as if the psycho-analyst whom the patient is attacking had a 'skin' which floated off him and now occupied some position between the psychoanalyst and the patient" (1967, p. 160).

The sphinx comes into being when thought, in its hunger for omni-science, seeks to convert the becoming of "O" into knowledge. This is the fundamental meaning of Oedipus's transgression; he fails to perceive that the intersection of the cross-roads, like a family tree, might restrain him from crossing certain boundaries. The reticulation arises like grace when thought, defeated by its omniscient cravings, is touched by the becoming of "O".

In order to discover how Bion relates the figure of the sphinx to the theme of reticulation, and to see how he was able to evolve the relationship into a more significant order, it is worth looking to another image, taken possibly from another patient (although it might be the same patient). We have to relate skin, reticulation, sphinx and primal water to a certain conception of clouds as premonitions of thought. Bion invokes the image of a "cloud of unknowing" from the writings of a mediaeval mystic. The cloud is made up of particles and is a form of reticulation.

In his paper "Attacks on Linking" (1959), Bion describes a patient who intuited a blue haze in the room one day, and on the next day intuited two shapes in the room which Bion called "probability clouds". Bion believed that the patient was hallucinating. At this stage in his thought, working within the medical vertex, Bion conceived of hallucination simply as a means of evacuating mental rubbish; he did not think of the hallucinating as a form of sign language that can enable functions of internalization as well as of evacuation—Bion had not yet linked hallucination to the influence of "O". Nor did he relate the haze or the two shapes to some apprehension of a gap that might have been idolized, or even iconicized.

Later in the same session the patient announced that a piece of iron had fallen to the floor. The patient entered into a series of convulsive movements which led, by way of an interpretation, to sensations in which he believed he was dying. (Was he falling into the void?)

Keeping to the medical vertex, Bion understood the clouds as marking the patient's attempt to eject a capacity for judgment which he had smashed into pieces; the patient wanted to eject his own smashed-up understanding of the therapist as a persecutor.

> His suspicion that the probability clouds were persecutory and hostile led him to doubt the value of guidance they afforded him... such as that a fact was an hallucination or vice versa... or would give rise to... delusions. The probability clouds themselves had some qualities of a primitive breast and were felt to be enigmatic and intimidating (1967, p. 100).

In a later book, *Elements of Psycho-Analysis* (1963), Bion's conception of probability clouds has begun to change. He no longer emphasizes their functions as representations of damage; he began to see them as evidence of insight into the unconscious syntax of the mind.

He relates them—by way of Elliott Jaques's (1959) theory that an unconscious reticulation, or schema, is the necessary ground to the capacity to work— to the sphinx in *Oedipus*, whose meaning in ancient Greek sphinx is "tight-binder". The ancient Greek understanding of riddles as being etymologically similar to woven rush-baskets heightens the parallel between failures in knowledge and qualities of reticulation (Onians, 1951, p. 369).[2]

At this stage in the evolution of his thought, Bion (1963) is concerned to see the clouds as factors in the symbolic transformations that occur on the threshold between the paranoid schizoid and depressive positions—as in Melanie Klein's formulation of the two positions. He writes of the clouds as made up of particles. The particles may come together, as depressive symbolization begins to take shape, or they may be fragmented and dispersed (p. 42).

Bion takes further the idea of probability clouds in *Transformations,* a book published in 1965. They are now like an understanding of skin as emanation. The confused nature of this image suggests that it requires the religious vertex to make sense of it. The medical vertex cannot categorize it.

Bion (1965) asks whether the "tension" of an idea in a session is able to appear visually as a probability cloud, or whether such a view is a form of thinking by metaphor. The distinction between hallucination and non-sensory intuition no longer has much application for him, in part because his attention is turned to the idea of pre-conception rather than to the idea of realization.

> As [the patient] lies on the couch and I sit [beside him], I imagine that a cloud begins to form rather in the way that clouds can sometimes be seen to form above a hot-point on a summer's day. It seems to be above him. A similar cloud may be visible to him, but he will see it arising from me. These are probability clouds (p. 117).

The clouds, like John Milton's rising world of waters, mark the first indications of the infinite as yielding up diaphanous and translucent forms.

Living within the medical vertex (which for much of the time I am happy to do), I may set too much store on the reassuring tactility of bodies. But the importance I attach to touch and to sensation as forms of knowledge and communication can result in an over-valuing of the idea of specificity in configuration—the idea that since I inhabit my body, as a people inhabits a country, I can lay claim to sovereignty over my body. To some extent, this is a fair claim. Reasonable people do not want to have their bodies violated. But you have to violate your body to the extent of submitting to Miltonic psychic blindness in order to see the truth. On this point mind is not bounded in the way that body is. The eyes of the mind are not constrained by the idea of Euclidean space.

Contact barrier theory presumes that all forms of space-time assertion are of variables perceived—if such a perception is possible—from the viewpoint of the void. I should say that this is *not* Bion's container theory, which belongs to the medical vertex. Indeed Bion's medical vertex theory of containment and his religious vertex theory of truth are incompatible yet inseparable. In order to survive as a therapist, the therapist has no choice but to respect the existence of both vertices in the consulting room.

NOTES

1. [Samuel] Johnson, who employed the term "metaphysical poets" [remarks] that "… the most heterogeneous ideas are yoked by violence together". The force of this impeachment lies in the failure of the conjunction, the fact that the ideas are yoked but not united…" (Eliot, 1921, in 1953, p. 283).
2. "Your account of the origin of the 'Sphinx' being a word meaning 'tight-binder,' and the link you made to a tightly-woven rush basket sparked a memory in me from childhood of a garden implement like a large-scale sieve, which in my family was called a 'riddle'. With the help of an etymological dictionary I now discover that this was not an idiosyncratic meaning but a late English usage. The dictionary meaning is given as 'A coarse meshed sieve used for separating chaff from corn, sand from gravel, ashes from cinders…' I wonder if the function of a riddle, which is designed to allow certain elements to pass through it and others not, sheds light on the contact barrier you spoke of" (Alf McFarland, private communication, 1994).
   A similar account is given for the fact that like comes together with like in Plato's *Timaeus*. Plato conceives of space as "a Recipient which affords a basis for images reflected in it, as in a mirror… Space is the 'room' or place where things are, not intervals or stretches of vacancy where things are not; and if he admits any void at all, it is only as the interstices which the particles cannot traverse (58a, B)… The notion of irregular particles rests on the simile of the winnowing-basket… woven of basketwork… a wide shovel-shaped basket, high at one end and flattened at the other, held by two handles projecting from the upper rim at the sides… The contrast is between the density and heaviness of the corn and the lightness and fine texture of the chaff. It is to these qualities that the separation of like to like is due, not to differences of shape or size. In the application, it is things of like quality that come together. These things are the 'vestiges' of fire and the rest, before any shape has been given to them" (Cornford, 1937, pp. 200-202). This description is suggestive of the particle constituents of the alpha and beta elements.

REFERENCES

Bick, E. (1968). The Experience of skin in early object relations. *Int. J. Psycho-Anal.*, 49: 484-486.
Bion, W.R. (1954). Notes on the Theory of Schizophrenia. *Int. J. Psycho-Anal.*, 35: 113-118. Also in: *Second Thoughts*. London: W. Heinemann, 1967, pp. 23-35.
—— (1958). On Arrogance. *Int. J. Psycho-Anal.*, 39:341-349. Also in: *Second Thoughts*, pp. 86-93.

Bion, W.R. (1959). Attacks on Linking. *Int. J. Psycho-Anal.*, 40: 308-315. Also in: *Second Thoughts*, pp. 93-109.

—— (1963). *Elements of Psycho-Analysis*. London: William Heinemann.

—— (1965). *Transformations*. London: William Heinemann.

—— (1967). *Second Thoughts*. London: William Heinemann.

—— (1970). *Attention and Interpretation*. London: Tavistock Publications.

—— (1973). *Brazilian Lectures 1*. Rio de Janeiro: Imago Editora. (Reprinted by Karnac Books in 1990.)

—— (1979). *A Memoir of the Future, Book Three: The Dawn of Oblivion*. Strath Tay: The Clunie Press.

Cornford, F.M. (1937). *Plato's Cosmology*. London: Kegan Paul.

Eliot, T.S. (1921). The Metaphysical Poets. Reprinted in: *Selected Essays* (1953 edition). London: Faber & Faber.

Empson, W. 1961. *Milton's God*. London: Chatto & Windus.

Fowler, H.W. (1948). *Dictionary of Modern English Usage*. Baltimore, MD: Omega Books.

Freud, S. (1915). The Unconscious. S.E., 14, pp. 159-215. In: J. Strachey (Ed.), *Standard Edition of the Complete Psychological Works of Sigmund Freud*, 24 volumes. London: Hogarth Press and The Institute of Psycho-Analysis, 1953-1974.

Jaques, E. (1959). Disturbances in the Capacity to Work. In: *Creativity and Work*, Madison, CT: International Universities Press, 1990.

Lovejoy, A.O. (1936). *The Great Chain of Being*. Cambridge, MA: Harvard University Press.

Meltzer, D., Bremner, J., Hoxter, S., Wedel, H., Wittenberg, I. (1975). *Explorations in Autism*. Strath Tay: The Clunie Press.

Onians, R.B. (1951). *Origins of European Thought*. Cambridge: Cambridge University Press.

28 Holland Park
London W11 3TA
England

CALL FOR PAPERS

The Journal of Melanie Klein & Object Relations cordially invites authors to submit papers for the following special issues:

THE PSYCHO-ANALYTICAL PROCESS BY DONALD MELTZER:
30 YEARS LATER

I. MATTE-BLANCO AND BI-LOGIC

PSYCHOANALYTIC PERSPECTIVES ON HATE

Contributors should send immediately a brief letter of interest, the title of their paper, and a summary of maximum 250 words. Send manuscripts to the Editor by *September 1, 1997*. All manuscripts should conform to the style of this publication (see "Instructions to Authors" in this issue, pp. 175-176).

* * *

CALL FOR COLLABORATION

For a volume tentatively titled

W.R. BION: AN INTERNATIONAL ANNOTATED BIBLIOGRAPHY

we need listings and brief summaries/descriptions of books, articles, studies, letters, photographs, recordings by and about the late Dr. Wilfred R. Bion. Authors fluent in German and Spanish are especially needed. Each author will be listed under the contributed entry. Mail or fax immediately letter of interest and inquiries to:

esf Publishers
Bion Biblio Project
1 Marine Midland Plaza
East Tower-Fourth Floor
Binghamton, New York 13901, USA
Fax: (607) 723-1401

WHEN DISCIPLINED DESCRIPTION PRECEDES INTERPRETATION: SLOWING DOWN MELTZER'S ACCOUNT OF *SINCERITY* TO REINSERT DESCRIPTION IN POST-KLEINIAN PHENOMENOLOGY

Maurice Apprey

The phenomenological psychological constitution of the phenomenon of "sincerity" has been determined. This determination was made by following the rigorous, classical phenenomenology of Edmund Husserl and a contemporary Husserlian psychological research praxis. In determining the phenomenological constitution of the phenomenon of sincerity, the author suggests that Meltzer's post-Kleinian account of the same phenomenon is legitimate even if he arrived at his results through a theory laden Kleinian psychoanalytic approach to interpretation rather than description. The present author, however, wants to show that when disciplined description precedes interpretation, Meltzer's account of sincerity can stand on much firmer ground and can no longer be dubbed precipitous or esoteric. In addition considerable detail has been gone into by the present author to illustrate to the reader precisely how Pinter's play, *The Dwarfs*, was unpacked to arrive at the inter-subjective constitution of sincerity so that even if the reader does not agree with the results, at least he or she might see how the outcome was achieved. Such a rigorous phenomenological praxis, then, is precisely what is needed, the author contends, as a necessary descriptive starting point before Meltzer's psychoanalytic interpretation is called upon to deepen the results of a descriptive study. Rigor then is fidelity to the human phenomenon under observation and not fixing ideas.

KEY WORDS. Edmund Husserl; Phenomenology; Description; Interpretation; Donald Meltzer; Harold Pinter; *The Dwarfs*; *The Birthday Party*; *The Homecoming*; Sincerity; and Amedeo Giorgi.

Introduction

In Donald Meltzer's *Sincerity* (Meltzer, 1994), a book-length phenomeno-logical account of the phenomenon of sincerity, he derived his findings by using three plays written by the British playwright Harold Pinter to serve as his data base. The three plays are *The Dwarfs* (1961), *The Birthday Party* (1959), and *The Homecoming* (1965). He exhorted the reader to join him in his clinical discussions on the phenomenon of sincerity with "a bit of method-ological agreement between author and reader.... The first requirement is that the reader must put this book [*Sincerity*] away... and not return to it until he has read [Pinter's] *The Dwarfs* at least once, preferably twice..." (Meltzer, 1994, p. 216). Then the reader is asked to read Meltzer's description of the latent content of *The Dwarfs*, re-read the play and finally join Meltzer again to explore the meanings and clinical implications and consequences of Meltzer's phenomenological account of the phenomenon of sincerity. The same procedure must be followed in exploring *The Birthday Party* and *The Homecoming*. Meltzer wants us to know that his reliance on Pinter's plays is not a commentary on the mental health of the writer but rather a testimony on "the artist whose powers of penetration and poetic description go far beyond my own [i.e., the psychoanalyst's], as scientist or as poet" (p. 187). Meltzer links Pinter's work in two directions: "psychologically with Freud's penetration of the dream and philosophically with Wittgenstein's penetra-tion of language games" (p. 187).

In my review of Meltzer's *Sincerity* (Apprey, 1996), I expressed my reservations on Meltzer's description of his work as phenomenological, suggesting that even though his work is phenomenologically inspired, his expositions are much too theory-laden to be phenomenological.

The primary purpose of this paper then is an attempt to insert descrip-tion back into Meltzer's phenomenology and in doing so I want to suggest one phenomenological praxis that can demonstrate that disciplined descrip-tion must precede interpretation when psychoanalytic researchers want to demonstrate that rigor is not fixing ideas but being faithful to an observable phenomenon.

I shall organize my project under four rubrics: (1) extracts from my review focussing on *Meltzer's account of the phenomenon of sincerity*; (2) the *phenomenological presence* and pre-conceptions that I bring to my account of Meltzer's work; (3) the relevant *phenomenological praxis* for explicitating the text provided by Pinter and the results attained when we heed Meltzer to read phenomenologically; and (4) discussion of the results in ways that *reinsert description* in a phenomenologically driven psychoanalytic account, thereby *suturing the gap created by precipitous interpretation*.

1. Meltzer's Account of the Phenomenon of Sincerity Derived from Pinter's *The Dwarfs, The Birthday Party,* and *The Homecoming*

According to Meltzer (1994), *The Dwarfs* is "a study in the organization of *infantile masculinity* in its *pregenital* aspects" that is "*struggling to free* itself from narcissistic collusion with the destructive part on the one hand and the sensual parasitic baby-part on the other" (p. 216; emphasis added). This struggle of the infantile pregenital masculinity to free itself from narcissistic collusion with destructive and parasitic infantile parts is hampered by three experiences:

> the suffering during separation from the mother from which pain it takes refuge in projective identification...; second, by its attempt at manic independence...; third, by its confusion about the reparative role of the father's penises inside the mother and difficulty to distinguish the good penis from Pete's faecal penis and the sensual part in projective identification with the good penis...; and finally by its own competition with these inside-penises in manic reparation... (*ibid.*, pp. 216-217).

For Meltzer, these obstacles to freeing the infantile organization caused by the mental pain of separation, manic independence, and zonal confusions "seem to form an exposition of *the nodal struggle between narcissism and object relations based upon the delicate balance between paranoid schizoid and depressive values*" (*ibid.*, p. 224; emphasis added). Such a nodal struggle between paranoid schizoid and depressive positions points in the direction of regressive or progressive values.

With respect to *The Birthday Party* as *a staging of regression into mental illness*, for Meltzer,

> the central fact is the *premorbid organization* of the personality at infantile levels *outside the depressive position*, still subject to a spectrum of confusions and still employing projective identification with internal objects as a refuge from mental pain and individual identity (*ibid.*, p. 228; emphasis added).

When projective identification with internal objects has been *employed* to abate the current of mental pain and when its use has been *fixed* in a consistent way as a result of overwhelming developmental processes at genital and pregenital levels, there is every opportunity for the *destructive parts* to *advance in their influence over other infantile structures.*

This destructive advance over the infantile structures proceeds by undermining the integrity of the good objects, creating confusion between good and bad internal objects as those destructive parts attempt to present themselves as benign. The advance of the destructive parts also proceeds by intrusively penetrating the claustrum, to which an infantile part has retreated as a consequence of projective identification. Thus, the destructive parts of the mind gain dominance over the regressed part of the infantile self-organization, eventually leading the regressed part away to *the unreal and delusional domain of the mind*.

Two broad categories of interference follow the delusional system. There may be *an inability to mean what one says* or an *incapacity to say what one means*. The first type of disorder of sincerity that shows when the subject is unable to mean what he says follows a particular narcissistic structure that at times presents as pseudo cooperation:

> that is, times when *an infantile structure* in projective identification with an internal object *presents itself* to the analyst *as if* it were the *adult* part of the patient. At such times, with certain more ill patients or ones with psychotic focus, the phenomenology described makes its appearance and may be observed by the analyst and *the adult of the patient*, as well, *if the latter* can be mobilized from its inertia (*ibid.*, p. 231; emphasis added).

Meltzer sees this kind of pseudo cooperation as an *un*sincerity that reflects *dishonesty*. In contrast to *unsincerity, or dishonesty*, there is a second type of problematic sincerity, where the subject is *unable to say what one means*. For this interference Meltzer reserves the term *insincerity*, which suggests "*incomplete sincerity*" (*ibid.*, p. 232). He suggest that, in its most florid form, insincerity *presents as catatonic mutism*, "*the ultimate catastrophe*" (*ibid.*, p. 232; emphasis added). In Meltzer's view, *there is a prisoner behind the blind stares*. In this interference, "*the destructive parts have captured the heterosexual infantile part within the claustrum of the internal mother's body and there hold it in-communicado*" (*ibid.*, p. 233; emphasis added). With the help of Pinter's *The Birthday Party*, Meltzer points to other pathological formations besides the blank stares of catatonia: "borderline patients, addicts, and perverts, in which it is *almost always the case that the heterosexuality is particularly poorly established* because of the withdrawal of that infantile part into massive *projective identification*" (*ibid.*, p. 237; emphasis added).

The use of massive projective identification is also implicated in *hypochondria*, where the question of what it means to know *who is in pain* is an intriguing one. In Meltzer's view, there is an *altering of the sense of identity when a subject employs the mechanism of projective identification*. In this situation, a part of the self *striving to escape infantile distress* enters an object but not without *expressing an identification with the object that now houses the split-off parts of the self*. To be precise, this experience of identification is not simply one of altered or changed identity. Rather, *the subject's identity is exchanged with that of the object.* The result of the exchange of identity in hypochondria tells us something about the *phenomenon of sincerity,* which, in that pathological formation, lies in the difficulty clinicians may meet in identifying the figure of representational object who is in pain: the damaged internal object or the subject who insincerely claims to be in pain. For Meltzer the example from hypochondria demonstrates

> the qualitative disturbance insincerity induced when the sense-of-identify is at the moment tied up with parts that are in a state of projective identifica-
> tion. *The irritating insincerity of the hypochondriac seems mysterious* until we recognize that... *we are annoyed because the person is claiming concern that really by rights should be directed to his damaged object* (ibid., p. 204; emphasis added).

If Pinter's *The Birthday Party* can help us make such distinctions between *un*sincerity, which manifests as dishonesty in a relative incapacity to mean what one says, and *in*sincerity, an incomplete capacity to say what one means, in the subject's retreat into mental illness, Pinter's *The Homecoming* points in the direction of positive mental health. This tilt toward positive mental health depends on the mechanism of introjective identification, from which the qualities of mind that favor greater sincerity emerge. When one depends on introjective identification, *"boastfulness gives way to humility; sadism yields to a sense of inferiority; sentimentality alters to passion; vanity metamorphoses into tenderness; and arrogance is replaced by a sense of responsibil-ity"* (ibid., p. 259; emphasis added). According to Meltzer, it is the analyst's task to try to understand the connection between these changes in mental state in terms of the quality of feelings and processes in integration in this self and object world.

2. Phenomenological Presence

There are three orienting assumptions behind the phenomenological presence that drives my project. I shall disclose them and then bracket or suspend my doxic theses before proceeding further with my project. The first is that description must precede interpretation. The second is that phenomenology can provide a particular kind of epistemology for psycho-analytic practice as the latter begins to participate fully in the epistemic conversation of postmodernism. Thirdly, if such a psychoanalytic phenom-enological account is feasible, it must provide an account of how an individual situates himself or herself in this world as well as a window into such larger issues as how humans negotiate historical narratives, cultural experiences of how bodies are colonized and/or emancipated. These three assumptions in part are backed by Kronfeld's view (1920):

> Phenomenology is a preliminary approach necessary for any psychological theory which seeks to explain phenomena (genetically); it is a preliminary approach in the same sense that any psychological ontology is. It is on the one hand the precondition for the formation of theories, and on the other hand it demands such theories; otherwise it remains essentially incomplete (p. 394).

Psychoanalytic thought, therefore can rely on phenomenology to delineate a platform for discovery and at the same time potentiate, after discovery from description, those phenomena that present themselves. In this way psychoanalysis may be in a better position to give up theories that appear to be a collection of anomalies in favor of a general theory.

When do these orienting assumptions find a place in today's psychoanalytic thought? Rustin (1991) has, inter alia, characterized the dimension of conception of theory as realist (Kleinian) or more phenomenological (post-Kleinian).

The three pretexts above would suggest that I must find a way to make complementarities out of antinomies. In other words to radicalize the realist position, I must include precisely what I want to radicalize by making it my starting point. Instead of dichotomies or ruptures, a post-Kleinian account, such as Meltzer's, can include a realist Kleinian account to avoid the charge of extremism. In this way (a) tendencies towards dichotomies of realism and phenomenology may be minimized or cor-rected, and (b) we may produce an epistemology that relies on circular causality rather than the linear causality that is implied in a realist, teleological account.

If description must follow interpretation, and if we are able to produce a particular kind of heuristic strategy that is circular, what is the clinical context for discovering, delineating, or creating this psychoanalytic ontology? We might begin by taking one phenomenological praxis to unpack Pinter's *The Dwarfs* to see what we will discover.

3. Phenomenological Psychological Praxis

Amedeo Giorgi, a phenomenological psychological researcher, followed Husserl, the father of phenomenological philosophy, in developing his phenomenological psychological research praxis. Let Giorgi (1979) speak for himself:

A brief description of the method is as follows: (1) The researcher reads the entire description of the... situation straight through to get a sense of the whole. (2) Next, the researcher reads the same description more slowly and delineates each time that a transition in meaning is perceived with respect to the intention of discovering the meaning of [the phenomenon under study]. After this procedure he has a series of meaning units or constituents. (3) The researcher then eliminates redundancies and clarifies or elaborates to himself the meaning of the units he just constituted by relating them to each other and to the sense of the whole. The researcher reflects on the given units, still expressed essentially in the concrete language of the subject, and comes up with the essence of that situation for the subject with respect to the phenomenon [under study]. Each unit is systematically interrogated for what it reveals about the [phenomenon] in that situation for that subject. The researcher transforms each unit, when relevant, into the language of psychological science. (4) The researcher synthesizes and integrates the insights achieved into a consistent description of the structure of [the phenomenon] (p. 83).

For the benefit of readers who are already familiar with Pinter's *The Dwarfs* or those who do not wish to follow every detail of how the following results were arrived at, I have transposed Steps 1, 2 and 3 of the praxis to the *Appendix*. Hopefully the format will render it more reader-friendly. Let us then proceed to the results of the study.

Step 4: Structure of Experience (Results of the Study)

In this domain of the mental world portrayed in *The Dwarfs*, a confined space of a hot oven, as it were, flowing milk is not available. What milk is there is stiff and caked in its bottle. Instead of flowing milk and honey, there are pickles, a toasting fork from anterior generations and from a far off strange place, and with a monkey head suggesting primitive and beastly longings. Breathing, in this place, is constricted and difficult. Hunger and thirst are not easily quenched. This chamber is compartmentalized so that *one alternately works on mental activities upstairs* and *eats downstairs*, particularly at night. This chamber of a hot oven provides access to vehicles which *come in and go out. Things can be carried back and forth. Hands can carry things back and forth*, but equally, *hands can carry out the work of assassins*. Thanks to assassins *there is always the threat of voicelessness, darkness, stillness, and all those manifestations which point to death as an inevitable ambush.*
In this chamber *one can stand in for another.* Limits and borders are imprecise and difficult to determine. *Things can enter the body by the wrong entrance* and stability is difficult to maintain. Nevertheless *rigidity and in-*

elasticity of mind renders one unable and unprepared to meet life's contingencies and deviations. Thus one may not be able to make appropriate distinctions such as those between what one smells and what one thinks. In this unstable world *the skin fails to hold a person's body self in place,* and therefore one's sense of oneself as an integrated whole does not even reflect in a mirror.

In the ambush toward death it is difficult to determine who controls whom, which part of self controls which, who bids an assassination, and who cleans up after a murder, because during assassinations, there are burnings, defecation into food, running wild, yowling, pinching, dribbling, whimpering, gouging, soothing of each participant's orifices with lotions, concealment of mess and decay with good scents.

This is a domain of *parasitism, avarice, enslavement and pus. In addition, there is a constellation of activities which include cannibalism, coprophagia and active killing of animals. Given these transgressions it is difficult to establish the identify of who one is and is not.* Difficult as it is to determine a sense of self and the limits of one's borders, *a conception of who one is does depend upon such contrivances and joint ventures between a person who perceives and one who is perceived. For identity, in this claustrum, is so fleeting and indeterminate that one cannot tell a surface description from an essence.* The inhabitants here are therefore trapped into a *forced mutuality* and *complicit involvement* with others which, here, constitute a simulation of friendship. This *contrived involvement* does not ameliorate desolation, starvation and the sense of abandonment. The good news, however, is that when carcass blends in with accumulated faecal droppings, their infusion into the land can potentially create manured fertile land which in turn may generate transformations into living flowers and shrubbery.

4. Discussion: Reinserting Description to Suture the Gap Caused by Interpretation

The structure of experience that constitutes our results comes remarkably close to Meltzer's (1966) account of the mental world described in an earlier paper on the connection between anal masturbation to the mechanism and process of projective identification. The proximity of our results to Meltzer's earlier account of anal masturbation and its relation to projective identification would suggest that Meltzer's intuitions and discoveries on the anal claustrum has a much longer history and precedes his book on *The Claustrum* (1992) by at least twenty-six years.

Let us revisit his earlier paper on anal masturbation and projective identification. There Meltzer (1966) tells us the following:

1. The domain of the anal claustrum is one of *pervasive sadism*.
2. There the atmosphere has a vertical structure of *abject tyranny* and submission that forebodes violence. Survival is the only value.
3. It is like a concentration camp with a diffuse terror of being dispensed with and in such a state there is profound loneliness in a bizarre world of *object presentations* where *representation is proscribed*.
4. Seen from the perspective of outside the object, the rectum of the internal mother houses the *debris* that is engendered by both the internal and external babies who cannot resist the impulse of fouling the maternal nest.
5. Seen from the inside, the rectum of the mother is *entered intrusively by stealth, intruded violently in anal masturbation or by anal assault* and is thus construed as a chamber where satanic religion is practiced; a chamber where the great faecal penis rules.
6. In this anal region *thoughtless assumptions are in vogue, considered thought proscribed*. Thus there is *conformity* in joining the leader of the faecal penis.
7. In this chamber *degradation, manipulation and dissimulation are rampant* and *acts of intimacy are non-existent*. Loyalty is dislocated by thoughtless devotion, trust is derailed by blind obedience, and excitement poses as emotion. *Guilt and the submission to punitive mandates replace regret*.
8. At length the inhabitants of this chamber *long for death*. This is essentially *a world of addiction* where the inhabitants have surrendered their survival to the whims of the ruling malignant objects.

It is as if the world depicted by Pinter's *The Dwarfs* and Meltzer's claustrum were interchangeable, at the very least horizonal. These two worlds depict *ruse, stealth, forced entry, simulation, dissimulation, contrivance, thoughtlessness* and do not appear to demonstrate a modicum of genuine attachment, concern, capacity for regret. This is, par excellence, a part object world.

Alberto Hahn (1994) stated that Meltzer mentioned the term "claustrum" for the first time in Meltzer's account of Harold Pinter's *The Birthday Party*. Our study here shows quite decisively that in addition to Meltzer's discovery of mental states that reveal various defects of the phenomenon of sincerity, Meltzer's discovery of the claustrum began with his account of Pinter's *The Dwarfs* but remained implicit. Thanks to the phenomenological process of explicitation, that is the journey from implicit to explicit, from darkness to light, as it were, the correspondence between Meltzer's earlier account of anal masturbation and his account of Pinter's *The Dwarfs* is incontrovertibly clear. *The correspondence between the two accounts shows, in at least the following areas of our part object mental world and here we can list them and show how the two descriptions of the world of The Dwarfs and that of the anal claustrum not only resemble one another but potentiate each other.*

The degraded life in both part object worlds then, makes it much clearer why a subject with defects in sincerity may be *unable to say what one means.* Here a *mindlessness* prevails and makes it impossible for a thoughtful mind to emerge from death, near-death, or variants of catatonic minds. In short, one cannot say what one means when one, as it were, has no mind or has a mind that possesses no stable or abiding shape of *its own. Mindlessness* comes to be horizonal with *in*sincerity.

Mindlessness as horizonal with *in*sincerity is a broader *configurational* theme and a necessary starting point for the purpose of reinserting description into Meltzer's phenomenology. To get to the next step of being in a situation where any phenomenological praxis can be transparent enough for us to see where an understanding of a phenomenon came from, even if we as readers did not agree with that understanding, let us go to some details that we might for convenience call *episodic themes.*

By episodic themes I am referring to Meltzer's translation into Kleinian thought of those particulars that include: playing the recorder as thumb-sucking, Len's retreating into Mark's house as projective identification, Earl's Court as a loss of difference between rectum and vagina, madness as elasticity.

Episode and configuration, however, go hand in hand. Parts interact with wholes. Accordingly, we can appeal to the Husserlian phenomenological strategy of returning to positivity, returning to beginnings, returning to the simplest things that stare us in the face but which we often miss because we are so busy interpreting into a tradition of metapsychological thought. In a sense we want to allow even those phenomena that appear to be anomalies to speak to us, to tell us that human nature reveals its bests ecrets through the exceptions. All this is a way of saying that we must make a transcendental turn from our findings and broaden our scope so that clinicians who are not psychoanalytically informed can see precisely what we see.

Meltzer has drawn our attention to the threat of Len's starvation and the intolerance of separation as motives for resorting to projective identification. How does one unpack this composite phenomenon in non-psychoanalytic terms? Let us go to what might initially seem like an unlikely source, the field of translation in comparative literature, particularly, the work of George Steiner, who wrote *After Babel* (1975). Here I am going to evoke the metaphor of colonization of one by another to link projective identification and the process of translating a text in order to make the transcendental turn. What Steiner writes of translation as a four-fold process is unwittingly synonymous with the process of projective identification. He suggests that the act of appropriative

The claustrum of 1966 ⟷ The claustrum of *The Dwarfs* in 1994

1. Suffocating heat in confinement and analogously chilling cold in confined spaces.

2. Artificial compartmentalization as if confusion would thus be avoided in a situation where *potential for death constitutes inevitable ambush.*

3. *Reversibility of roles* of persons is in vogue.

4. *Permeability* of borders so that wrong entrances may be entered in frenzied actions.

5. *Elasticity of borders* succumbs to rigidity of wills, impulses, thrusts, actions of its subjects.

6. The skin is but a facade; surfaces and essences are thus interchangeable. The skins fades easily so that it peels willingly upon encounter with an other; faces of subjects cannot reflect a surface backed by the taint of a mirror. The result is a composite set of behaviors of simulation, complicit involvements, feigned mutuality or reciprocity that seem to stand in for parasitism, sadism, *coprophagic impulses of killing greed,* etc.

1. *Sadism.*

2. Abject tyranny of the atmosphere of a *concentration camp* where concrete *presentations operate,* representations proscribed.

3. *Entrances* of otherwise *proximal but separate* places *are collapsible and permeable.*

4. Thoughtlessness prevailing and leading to *blind conformity.*

5. Intimacy does not exist; *deception, degradation, simulation prevail.*

6. Participants *long for death.*

transfer of meaning is fourfold: (a) initiative trust, (b) aggressive penetration, (c) incorporative embodiment, and (d) restitution. In regard to the first process, Steiner (1975) writes, "There is an initiative trust, an investment of belief... We venture a leap: we grant ab initio that there is 'something there' to be understood, that *the transfer will not be void"* (p. 297). After this confiding trust in the author/text comes aggression; a process of "understanding as an act, on the access, inherently appropriative and therefore violent" (*ibid.,* p. 297). There is the Hegelian postulate here that "all cognition is aggressive, that every proposition is an *inroad* on the world" (*ibid.,* p. 297). After the penetrative movement of incorporation in Steiner's fourfold hermeneia comes embodiment. He writes:

> The third movement is incorporative, in the strong sense of the word. The import, of meaning and of form, the embodiment is not made into a vacuum. The native semantic field is already extant and crowded. There are innumerable shadings of assimilation and placement of the newly acquired, ranging from a complete domestication, an at-homeness at the core...The Heideggerian "we are what we understand to be" entails that our own being is modified by each occurrence of comprehensive appropriation. No language, no traditional symbolic set or cultural ensemble imports without risk of being transformed (*ibid.,* pp. 298-299).

The self-in-the-other, as it were, is yoked with the one who houses it. However, there is the risk that the self may be consumed. The balancing act of exchange and restoration must occur. This balancing act is the work of the fourth process of restitution. In this last sequence of the fourfold hermeneia,

> We encircle and invade cognitively. We come home laden, thus again off-balance, having caused disequilibrium throughout the system by taking away from "the other" and by adding, though possibly with ambiguous consequence, to our own. The system is now off-tilt. The hermeneutic act must compensate. If it is to be authentic, it must mediate into exchange and restored parity (*ibid.,* p. 300).

Here is an act of reciprocity whose function is to restore balance. Potentially, then, there could be loss of self in the other, and/or breakage in the other, and for that reason the self in the other must now compensate, and it does so by inducing a new cycle of reaching out of the other only to begin the process of thrusting the self into an other all over again.

Pinter's Len, Meltzer's baby, as it were, under the threat of starvation and intolerance of separation must find asylum in a place whose owner he can *colonize and confide in.* In this sense the initiative trust is synonymous with seeking *a suitable object of projection.* Unfortunately, Mark's own sensual needs cannot allow him to feed Len, the baby, in the way he asks to be fed, that is, by mouth. Rather, he has available to him a feed of semen through the phallus by the wrong entrance, the unexpected orifice of the anus, the chamber of suffocation, leading to a claustrophobic ambush. The suffocating heat in turn erodes borders, peels the skin of the inhabitants in the chamber. With indeterminate borders, roles are reversible. When no sense of self exists, no borders will stay on. Accordingly, there is no sense of order. Tyranny follows. With tyranny comes mindlessness and degradation. With degradation and mindlessness, comes destruction and/or death. It is in this context that stiff milk in a bottle and gherkins in place of milk is construed as semen in the rectum due to zonal confusion. The breast/top/mouth constellation should receive milk but rather the bottom receives it. Besides, it is not the front bottom that receives the semen; rather it is the back bottom that receives the phallus (gentleman's man).

Invoking then Steiner's categories of translation/colonization, Len in an initiative trust confides in Mark to deal with his mental pain of intolerance of separation and starvation. Instead, he finds the phallus that penetrates rectally. The result is that he stores the semen in a state of incorporative embodiment. Now, in restitutive transfer, we have lost sight of the originary mouth only to see a drama of exchange between top and bottom orifices.

With regard to zonal confusions, the mental picture of Earl's Court as a place for "actors," that is, people who stand in for others, also comes by inference to mean a place for prostitutes, that is, people who stand in for others (Latin, "prostituere," to stand in for). Meltzer's translation of Earl's Court in *The Dwarfs* is that "the penis does not know the difference between rectum and vagina" (Meltzer, 1994, p. 218). In this respect the rectum is a stand-in for the vagina. In a world of stand-ins, boundaries will be imprecise. Elasticity will prevail. Hence the peeling of skins in ways where there is no reflection of self and/or other, further erosion of borders, the establishment of disorder, tyranny of the phallic assassins, degradation, and death. The point here is that all the episodic themes of projective identifications, boundary-lessness, unctuation of the rectum, replacement of part-object functions are not arbitrary translations by Meltzer but part-object activity that converges into the "mind-lessness," destruction, and death in the chamber, the anal claustrum.

If this account of explicitation of Meltzer's work seems repetitive, this repetitiveness is part of the tedious work that must be done to unpack what may be misread as precipitous interpretation in Meltzer's work. Thanks to a Husserlian phenomenological praxis, we may be able, then, to show that when disciplined description precedes interpretation, Meltzer's phenomenologically inspired metapsychology may no longer be dubbed "esoteric" with any legitimacy.

APPENDIX: **PINTER'S *THE DWARFS*[1]**
AND **PHENOMENOLOGICAL STEPS 1-3**[2]

[....]

1. [LEN *is playing a recorder. The sound is fragmentary.*]

    LEN: Pete.

    PETE: What?

    LEN: Come here.

    PETE: What?

    LEN: What's the matter with this recorder? [*He pulls recorder in half, looks down, blows, taps.*] There's something wrong with this recorder./

{1. Subject L (len) frets over his situation when his musical instrument, a recorder, fails to work to his liking.}

2. PETE: Let's have some tea./

{2. Subject P (Pete), in contrast, wants to drink, wants to have tea.}

3. LEN: I can't do a thing with it.
           [*Re-assembles recorder. Another attempt to play.*]
           Where's the milk?
           [*He puts recorder on tray.*]/

{3. S(L) continues to fret over his broken recorder and now joins S(P) to fret over the absence of milk.}

4. PETE: You were going to bring it.

    LEN: That's right.

    PETE: Well, where is it?

    LEN: I forgot it. Why didn't you remind me?/

{4. Ss (L and P) ponder whose responsibility it is for the absence of milk and L owns up to his responsibility for the absence of milk when he admits that his memory failed him.}

5. PETE: Give me the cup.

LEN: What do we do now?/

{5. S(P) demands a cup while S(L) wonders what they could do without milk.}

6. PETE: Give me the tea.
    LEN: Without milk?
    PETE: There isn't any milk./

{6. S(P) demands tea without milk to S L's surprise.}

7. LEN: What about sugar? [*Moving towards door.*] He must have a pint of milk somewhere. [*He exits to kitchen. Noise of opening cupboards, etc. He reappears with a couple of gherkins in a jar.*] Here's a couple of gherkins. What about the gherkin? [*Takes jar to* PETE.] Fancy a gherkin. [PETE *sniffs, looks up in disgust.* LEN *sniffs and exits.*] Wait a minute. [*Kitchen noises.* LEN *reappears with a bottle of milk.*] Ah! Here we are. I knew he'd have a pint laid on. [*Pressing the top.*] Uuh! Uuuhh.... It's stiff.
    PETE: I wouldn't open that.
    LEN: Uuhh... why not? I can't drink tea without milk. Uuh! That's it. [*Picking up cup to pour.*] Give us your cup.
    PETE: Leave it alone.
              [*Pause.* LEN *shakes bottle over cup.*]/

{7. S(L) searches Subject M (Mark's) kitchen, readily finds and brings forth a couple of pickles to S(P) who receives L's gesture with disgust. In a further effort S(L) discovers milk, stiff milk that cannot flow.}

8. LEN: It won't come out. [*Pause.*] The milk won't come out of the bottle.
    PETE: It's been in there two weeks, why should it come out?
    LEN: Two weeks? He's been away longer than two weeks. [*Slight pause.*] It's stuck in the bottle. [*Slight pause.*] You'd think a man like him would have a maid, wouldn't you, to look after the place while he's away, to look after his milk? Or a gentleman. A gentleman's gentleman. Are you quite sure he hasn't got a gentleman's gentleman tucked away somewhere, to look after the place for him?/

{8. S(L) regrets the milk will not flow from the bottle while S(P) explains that the caretaker of the milk, S(M), has been away longer than two weeks. In the view of S(L), S(M) has neglected his caretaking duty over having to make milk available and preserving good milk. Accordingly S(L) protests that S(M) has no maid to ensure the flow of milk and wishfully yearns for an alternative of a male housekeeper to perform housekeeping duties even if such a male housekeeper is hidden from observation.}

9. PETE [*Rising to replace book on shelf:*] Only you. You're the only gentleman's gentleman he's got.
[*Pause.*]

LEN: Well, if I'm his gentleman's gentleman, I should have been looking after the place for him.
[*Pause.* PETE *takes brass toasting fork off wall.*]/

{9. S(P) putting a book back in its rightful place tells S(L) that S(L) is the soulmate of the man that S(M) has got; a reminder which S(L) accepts with guilt and resignation.}

10. PETE: What's this?
    LEN: That? You've seen that before. It's a toasting fork.
    PETE: It's got a monkey's head.
    LEN: It's Portuguese. Everything in this house is Portuguese.
    PETE: Why's that?/

{10. S(P) discovers on S's (M's) wall an unusual instrument, toasting fork with a monkey's head and whose origin is Portuguese; a curious looking instrument for stirring a fireplace but which conjures up an image of animal symbolism and strange origins.}

11. LEN: That's where he comes from.
    PETE: Does he?
    LEN: Or at least, his grandmother on his father's side. That's where the family comes from.
    PETE: Well, well.
    [*He hangs up the toasting fork.*]/

{11. Ss (L and P) settle on the assumption that the potentially hot instrument for stirring a fireplace has animal symbolism, comes from strange places of origin and in addition was passed down from anterior generations through S's (M's) father's mother.}

12. LEN: What time's he coming?
    PETE: Soon.
    [*He pours himself a cup of tea.*]/

{12. S(L) longs for S(M).}

13. LEN: You're drinking black tea.
    PETE: What about it?
    LEN: You're not in Poland.
    [*He plays recorder.* PETE *sits in armchair.*]/

{13. S(L) protests that S(P) is drinking tea without milk as though such a behavior only belongs elsewhere.}

14. PETE: What's the matter with that thing?
    LEN: Nothing. There's nothing wrong with it. But it must be broken. It's a year since I played it. [*He sneezes.*] Aah! I've got the most shocking blasted cold I've ever had in all my life. [*He blows his nose.*] Still, it's not much of a nuisance really./

{14. S(P) wonders what could be wrong with S's (L's) recorder and learns that S(L) has not played the recorder for a whole year and besides S(L) has a most severe and constricting cold.}

15. PETE: Don't wear me out. [*Slight pause.*] Why don't you pull yourself together? You'll be ready for the loony bin next week if you go on like this.
    [LEN *uses recorder as a telescope to the back of* PETE'S *head.*]
    [*Pause.*]/

{15. S(P) anticipates that S(L) is becoming mentally deranged.}

16. LEN: Ten to one he'll be hungry.
    PETE: Who?
    LEN: Mark. When he comes. He can eat like a bullock, that bloke. Still, he won't find much to come home to, will he? There's nothing in the kitchen, there's not even a bit of lettuce. It's like the workhouse here. [*Pause.*] He can eat like a bullock, that bloke. [*Pause.*] I've seen him finish off a loaf of bread before I'd got my jacket off [*Pause.*] He'd never leave a breadcrumb on a plate in the old days. [*Pause.*] Of course, he may have changed. Things do change. But I'm the same. Do you know, I had five solid square meals one day last week? At eleven o'clock, two o'clock, six o'clock, ten o'clock, and one o'clock. Not bad going. Work makes me hungry. I was working that day. [*Pause.*] I'm always starving when I get up. Daylight has a funny effect on me. As for the night, that goes without saying. As far as I'm concerned the only thing you can do in the night is eat. It keeps me fat, especially if I'm at home. I have to run downstairs to put the kettle on, run upstairs to finish what I'm doing, run downstairs to cut a sandwich or arrange a salad, run upstairs to finish what I'm doing, run back downstairs to see to the sausages, if I'm having sausages, run back upstairs to finish what I'm doing, run back downstairs to lay the table, run back upstairs to finish what I'm

doing, run back—
PETE: Yes!/

{16. S(P), hungry and thirsty enough to have black tea, that is, tea without milk anticipates that, like him S(M), whose house has stiff milk and pickles and an unusual fire
toaster from a far will be quite hungry upon his return home. It is as if one hungry man
knows an other's hunger well enough to have the same cast of mind or to exchange
each other's experience of starvation. Such an abiding starvation cannot be sated by the
exercise of continually running upstairs and downstairs at night and between cooking
and eating sandwiches and sausages downstairs, and working upstairs.}

17. LEN: Where did you get those shoes?
    PETE: What?
    LEN: Those shoes. How long have you had them?
    PETE: What's the matter with them?
    LEN: Have you been wearing them all night?
          [*Pause.*]/

{17. S(L) wonders if S(P) has been wearing shoes all night, staying up all night, as it
were.}

18. PETE: When did you last sleep?
          [*His hand is lying open, palm upward.*]
    LEN: Sleep? Don't make me laugh. All I do is sleep./

{18. S(P) wonders in return when S(L) slept and finds out that S(L) sleeps all the time
in contrast to S(P) who goes up and down at night between working upstairs and eating
downstairs.}

19. PETE: What about work? How's work?
    LEN: Paddington? It's a big railway station. An oven. It's an oven. Still,
          bad air is better than no air. It's best on night shift. The trains come
          in, I give a bloke half a dollar, he does my job. I curl up in the corner
          and read the timetables. But they tell me I might make a first class
          porter. I've been told I've got the makings of a number one porter.
          What are you doing with your hand?/

{19. If S(P) works upstairs and eats downstairs, S(L) works at a very busy railway
station where trains come and go, creating a hot and asphyxiating station and he solves
that problem by bribing someone to do his work in the oven of a station so that he can
rest idly in a corner. S(L) hears that he can make a first class porter, one who carries
things back and forth.}

20. PETE: What are you talking about?
    LEN: What are you doing with your hand?
    PETE: [*Coolly:*] What do you think I'm doing with it? Eh? What do you think?
    LEN: I don't know.
    PETE: I'll tell you, shall I? Nothing. I'm not doing anything with it. It's not moving. I'm doing nothing with it.
    LEN: You're holding it palm upwards.
    PETE: What about it?
    LEN: It's not normal. Let's have a look at that hand. Let's have a look at it. [*Pause. He gasps through his teeth.*] You're a homicidal maniac.
    PETE: Is that a fact?
    LEN: Look. Look at that hand. Look, look at it. A straight line across the middle. Right across the middle, see? Horizontal. That's all you've got. What else have you got? You're a nut.
    PETE: Oh yes?
    LEN: You couldn't find two men in a million with a hand like that. It sticks out a mile. A mile. That's what you are, that's exactly what you are, you're a homicidal maniac!
    [*A knock on the outer door.*]/

{20. S(L) perceives that S(P) is doing something ominous with his hands, that a straight line across his hand points to all the makings of an assassin, a homicidal maniac.}

21. PETE [*Rising to exit:*] That's him. [*He goes off. The lights begin to fade to blackout.*]
    MARK: [*Off.*] Anyone here?
    PETE: [*Off.*] Yes, how are you?
    MARK: [*Off.*] Any tea?
    PETE: [*Off.*] Polish tea.
    [*Blackout. The lights come up in* LEN'S *room—overhead lamp.* LEN *is sitting at the side of the table.*]/

{21. S(P) notices that S(M), the houseowner has arrived. S(M) wastes no time in asking if tea is available; a request anticipated by S(P) who sees S(M) as one who eats like a bullock.}

22. LEN: There is my table. That is a table. There is my chair. There is my table. That is a bowl of fruit. There is my chair. There are my curtains. There is no wind. It is past night and before morning. This is my room. This is a room. There is a wall-paper, on the walls. There are six walls. Eight walls. An octagon. This room is an octagon.

There are my shoes, on my feet. This is a journey and an ambush. This is the centre of the cold, a halt to the journey and no ambush. This is the deep grass I keep to. This is the thicket in the centre of the night and the morning. There is my hundred watt bulb like a dagger. This room moves. This room is moving. It has moved. It has reached... a dead halt. This is my fixture. There is no web. All's clear and abundant. Perhaps a morning will arrive. If a morning arrives, it will not destroy my fixture, nor my luxury. If it is dark in the night or light, nothing obtrudes. I have my compartment. I am wedged. Here is my arrangement, and my kingdom. There are no voices. They make no hole in my side.

[*The doorbell rings.* LEN *searches for his glasses on the table, rummaging among the books. Lights tablecloth. Is still. Searches in armchair. Then on mantlepiece. Bell rings again. He searches under table. Bell rings again. He rises, looks down, sees glasses in top pocket of jacket. Smiles, puts them on. Exits to open front door.* MARK *enters to below table.* LEN *follows.*]/

{22. S(L) senses a deadend, a dead halt in his his life; a state of mind where he fears a still fixure and bracing himself for that perceived eventuality of voicelessness, darkness, stillness, and death, he anchors himself by naming the objects, things, in his surroundings as though naming things can keep him from his journey towards an inevitable ambush and death.}

23. LEN: What's this, a suit? Where's your carnation?
MARK: What do you think of it?
LEN: It's not a schmutta.
MARK: It's got a zip at the hips.
LEN: A zip at the hips? What for?
MARK: Instead of a buckle. It's neat.
LEN: Neat? I should say it's neat.
MARK: No turn-ups.
LEN: I can see that. Why didn't you have turn-ups?
MARK: It's smarter without turn-ups.
LEN: Of course it's smarter without turn-ups.
MARK: I didn't want it double-breasted.
LEN: Double-breasted? Of course you couldn't have it double-breasted.
MARK: What do you think of the cloth?
LEN: The cloth? [*He examines it, gasps and whistles through his teeth. At a great pace.*] What a piece of cloth. What a piece of cloth. What a piece of cloth. What a piece of *cloth*.
MARK: You like the cloth?
LEN: What a piece of CLOTH!

MARK: What do you think of the cut?

LEN: What do I think of the cut? The cut? The cut? What a cut! What a cut! I've never seen such a cut! [*Pause.*] [*He sits and groans.*]

MARK [*combing his hair and sitting*] : Do you know where I've just been?

LEN: Where?

MARK: Earl's Court.

LEN: Uuuuhh! What were you doing there? That's beside the point./

{23. S(M) shows S(L) his new suit and seeks affirmation for his taste of clothing with new style items: a zip instead of buckle, no turn-ups, single-breasted jacket but gets no positive strokes, only more quizzical remarks.}

24. MARK: What's the matter with Earl's Court?

LEN: It's a mortuary without a corpse. [*Pause.*] There's a time and place for everything...

MARK: You're right there.

LEN: What do you mean by that?

MARK: There's a time and place for everything.

LEN: You're right there. [*Puts glasses on, rises to* MARK.] Who have you been with? Actors and actresses? What's it like when you act? Does it please you? Does it please anyone else?

MARK: What's wrong with acting?

LEN: It's a time-honoured profession—it's time-honoured. [*Pause.*] But what does it do? Does it please you when you walk onto a stage and everybody looks up and watches you? Maybe they don't want to watch you at all. Maybe they'd prefer to watch someone else. Have you every asked them? [MARK *chuckles.*] You should follow any example and take up mathematics. [*Showing him open book.*] Look! All last night I was working at mechanics and determinants. There's nothing like a bit of calculus to cheer you up. [*Pause.*]/

{24. S(L) seeks S(M)'s visit to Earl's Court as a visit to a place where there is death in life, a mortuary without a corpse and sees S(M)'s companions in Earl's Court as actors and actresses in an old profession where humans stand in for others. In his S(L)'s view one must work on concrete descriptions of things as they are rather than flirting with people who prostitute themselves, that is act as stand-ins for others for in death one can play a role and not see oneself.}

25. MARK: I'll think about it.

LEN: Have you got a telephone here?

MARK: It's your house.

LEN: Yes. What are you doing here? What do you want here?

MARK: I thought you might give me some bread and honey.

LEN: I don't want you to become too curious in this room. There's no place
       for curiosities here. Keep a sense of proportion. That's all I ask.

MARK: That's all./

{25. S(M) seeks a feed of "bread and honey" in addition to the milk he had asked for
before and is admonished by S(L) to keep a sense of proportion and not to seek
excesses.}

26. LEN: I've got enough on my plate with this room as it is.

    MARK: What's the matter with it?

    LEN: The rooms we live in... open and shut. [*Pause.*] Can't you see? They
           change shape at their own will. I wouldn't grumble if only they
           would keep to some consistency. But they don't. And I can't tell the
           limits, the boundaries, which I've been led to believe are natural. I'm
           all for the natural behaviour of rooms, doors, staircases, the lot. But
           I can't rely on them. When, for example, I look through a train
           window, at night, and see the yellow lights, very clearly, I can see
           what they are, and I see that they're still. But they're only still
           because I'm moving. I know that they do move along with me, and
           when we go round a bend, they bump off. But I know that they are
           still, just the same. They are, after all, stuck on poles which are
           rooted to the earth. So they must be still, in their own right, insofar
           as the earth itself is still, which of course it isn't. The point is, in a
           nutshell, that I can only appreciate such facts when I'm moving.
           When I'm still nothing around me follows a natural course of
           conduct. I'm not saying I'm any criterion, I wouldn't say that. After
           all, when I'm on the train I'm not really moving at all. That's obvi-
           ous. I'm in the corner seat. I'm still. I am perhaps being moved, but
           I do not move. Neither do the yellow lights. The train moves,
           granted, but what's a train got to do with it?

    MARK: Nothing./

{26. S(L) is preoccupied with the changing experience of him in a situation where the
room he is in opens and shuts and threatens to shut him in so that he cannot tell
where limits and boundaries are. As a result nothing around him follows any natural
course of conduct and when borders are imprecise one does not know when one
moves under one's own volition and when one is moved by an other force.}

27. LEN: You're frightened.

    MARK: Am I?

    LEN: You're frightened that any moment I'm liable to put a red hot burning coal in your mouth.

MARK: Am I?

LEN: But when the times comes, you see, what I shall do is place the red hot burning coal in my own mouth.
[*Swift blackout.* PETE *sits where* MARK *has been. Lights snap up.*]
I've got some beigels. /

{27. S(L) senses that S(M) is frightened by S(L)'s changing world and suggests that a change in S(L)'s world might prompt S(L) to put hot burning coal in S(M)'s mouth as if to say that when one's mind changes one may put a burning sensation in the wrong place, in another person's mouth when in fact S(L)'s reality is that when his mind changes he is more likely to put the burning object in his own mouth.}

28. PETE: This is a very solid table, isn't it?

LEN: I said I've got some beigels.

PETE: No thanks. How long have you had this table?

LEN: It's a family heirloom.

PETE: Yes, I'd like a good table, and a good chair. Solid stuff. Made for the bearer. I'd put them in a boat. Sail it down the river. A houseboat. You could sit in the cabin and look out at the water.

LEN: Who'd be steering?

PETE: You could park it. Park it. There's not a soul in sight.

LEN *brings half full bottle of wine and glass to table. Reads label. Sniffs at bottle. Pours some into glass, savours then gargles, walking about. Spits wine back into glass, returns bottle and glass at sideboard, after a defensive glance at* PETE. *Returns to above table.*

LEN: [*Muttering:*] Impossible, impossible, impossible. /

{28. S(P) wishes he had solid furniture, one that is solid enough to locate a houseboat that moves on water and in this way one may seek and find stability on land and on water.}

29. PETE: [*Briskly:*] I've been thinking about you.

LEN: Oh?

PETE: Do you know what your trouble is? You're not elastic. There's no elasticity in you. You want to be more elastic.

LEN: Elastic? Elastic. Yes, you're quite right. Elastic. What are you talking about?

PETE: Giving up the ghost isn't so much a failure as a tactical error. By elastic I mean being prepared for your own deviations. You don't know where you're going to come out next at the moment. You're like a rotten old shirt. Buck your ideas up. They'll lock you up before you're much older. /

{29. S(P) proclaims that when one is fixed in one's mind, when one is not elastic enough one may not be spared for contingencies and deviations and thus may become mentally disturbed.}

30. LEN: No. There is a different sky each time I look. The clouds run about in my eye. I can't do it.

PETE: The apprehension of experience must obviously be dependent upon discrimination if it's to be considered valuable. That's what you lack. You've got no idea how to preserve a distance between what you smell and what you think about it. You haven't got the faculty for making a simple distinction between one thing and another. Every time you walk out of this door you go straight over a cliff. What you've got to do is nourish the power of assessment. How can you hope to assess and verify anything if you walk about with your nose stuck between your feet all day long? You knock around with Mark too much. He can't do you any good. I know how to handle him. But I don't think he's your sort. Between you and me, I sometimes think he's a man of weeds. Sometimes I think he's just playing a game. But what game? I like him all right when you come down to it. We're old pals. But you look at him and what do you see? An attitude. Has it substance or is it barren? Sometimes I think it's as barren as a bombed site. He'll be a spent force in no time if he doesn't watch his step. [*Pause.*] I'll tell you a dream I had last night. I was with a girl in a tube station, on the platform. People were rushing about. There was some sort of panic. When I looked around I saw everyone's faces were peeling, blotched, blistered. People were screaming, booming down the tunnels. There was a fare bell clanging. When I looked at the girl I saw that her face was coming off in slabs too, like plaster. Black scabs and stains. The skin was dropping off like lumps of cat's meat. I could hear it sizzling on the electric rails. I pulled her by the arm to get her out of there. She wouldn't budge. Stood there, with half a face, staring at me. I screamed at her to come away. Then I thought, Christ, what's my face like? Is that why she's staring? Is that rotting too?

Lights change. LEN'S *room.* PETE *and* MARK *looking at chess board.* LEN *watching them. Silence. /*

{30. Against the background of S(L)'s rigidity, S(P) perceives that one is in danger of deteriorating in one's mind when one does not or cannot discriminate between what one smells and what one thinks. Equally, one endangers oneself when one relates to a person who has no depth and presents as superficial, sensuous, and barren. The greatest danger, however, shows itself when the border between persons breaks down and the skin that holds a person in one's body fails to mark the boundaries of humans.}

31. LEN: Eh...
    [*They don't look up.*]
    The dwarfs are back on the job. [*Pause.*] I said the dwarfs are back on the job.
MARK: The what?
LEN: The dwarfs.
MARK: Oh yea?
LEN: Oh yes. They've been waiting for a smoke signal you see. I've just sent up the smoke signal.
    [*Pause.*]
MARK: You've just sent it up, have you?
LEN: Yes. I've called them in on the job. They've taken up their positions. Haven't you noticed?
PETE: I haven't noticed. [*To* MARK.] Have you noticed?
    MARK *chuckles.*
LEN: But I'll tell you one thing. They don't stop work until the job in hand is finished, one way or another. They never run out on a job. Oh no. They're true professionals. Real professionals.
PETE: Listen. Can't you see we're trying to play chess?
    [*Pause.*]
LEN: I've called them in to keep an eye on you two, you see. They're going to keep a very close eye on you. So am I. We're waiting for you to show your hand. We're all going to keep a very close eye on you two. Me and the dwarfs.
    [*Pause.*]
MARK: [*Referring to chess:*] I think I've got you knackered, Pete.
    [PETE *looks at him.*]
PETE: Do you?

Lights change and come up full in MARK'S *room.* LEN *enters with old gilt mirror,* MARK *follows.* /

{31. S(L) now names the dwarfs as the real, efficient and professional assassins who never run out of a job and remain circumspect until the job is done.}

32. MARK: Put that mirror back.

    LEN: This is the best piece of furniture you've got in the house. It's Spanish. No Portuguese. You're Portuguese, aren't you?

    MARK: Put it back.

    LEN: Look at your face in this mirror. Look. It's a farce. Where are your features? You haven't got any features. You couldn't call those features. What are you going to do about it, eh? What's the answer?

    MARK: Mind that mirror. It's not insured.

    LEN: I saw Pete the other day. In the evening. You didn't know that. I wonder about you. I often wonder about you. But I must keep pedalling. I must. There's a time limit. Who have you got hiding here? You're not alone here. What about your Esperanto? Don't forget, anything over two ounces goes up a penny.

    MARK: Thanks for the tip.

    LEN: Here's you mirror.

> MARK *exits with mirror.* LEN *picks out apple from a fruit bowl, sits in armchair staring at it.* MARK *returns./*

{32. For S(L) one must have clear and definable features which show in a mirror. In addition to features needing to be demonstrable, no other person must be hidden from him in the house, nor should any foreign language be hidden from him.}

33:      This is a funny-looking apple.

        [*He tosses it back to* MARK, *who replaces it.*]

        Pete asked me to lend him a shilling.

    MARK: Uh?

    LEN: I refused.

    MARK: What?

    LEN: I refused downright to lend him a shilling.

    MARK: What did he say to that?

    LEN: Plenty. Since I left him I've been thinking thoughts I've never thought before. I've been thinking thoughts I've never thought before.

    MARK: You spend too much time with Pete.

    LEN: What?

    MARK: Give it a rest. He doesn't do you any good. I'm the only one who knows how to get on with him. I can handle him. You can't. You take him too seriously. He doesn't worry me. I know how to handle him. He doesn't take any liberties with me.

    LEN: Who says he takes liberties with me? Nobody takes liberties with me. I'm not the sort of man you can take liberties with.

MARK: You should drop it./

{33. S(L) recognizes that since he left S(M) he has been thinking thoughts he has not thought before.}

34.   LEN *sees toasting fork, takes it to* MARK.
   LEN: This is a funny toasting fork. Do you ever make any toast?
            He drops the fork on the floor.
            Don't touch it! You don't know what will happen if you touch it! You
            mustn't touch it! You mustn't bend! Wait. [*Pause.*] I'll bend. I'll... pick
            it up. I'm going to touch it. [*Pause... softly.*] There. You see? Nothing
            happens when I touch it. Nothing. Nothing can happen. No one
            would bother. [*A broken sigh.*] You see, I can't see the broken glass. I
            can't see the mirror. I have to look through. I see the other side. The
            other side. But I can't see the mirror side. [*Pause.*] I want to break it,
            all of it. But how can I break it? How can I break it when I can't see
            it?

            Lights fade and come up again in MARK'S *room.* LEN *is sitting in an*
            armchair. MARK *enters with whisky bottle and two glasses. He pours drinks*
            for PETE *and himself.* PETE, *who has followed him in, takes his glass.* MARK
            sits in other armchair. Neither take any notice of LEN.
            Silence./

{34. S(L) converses with himself about the toasting fork, wondering if it will hurt him
if he touches or bends it and does touch it only to conclude that it is harmless. But
then, in almost the same breath, he concludes that he sees the tain of the mirror which
does not reflect his features. In the tain of the mirror the self is not reflected.}

35. PETE: Thinking got me into this and thinking's got to get me out. You
            know what I want? An efficient idea. You know what I mean? An
            efficient idea. One that'll work. Something I can pin my money on.
            An each way bet. Nothing's guaranteed, I know that. But I'm willing
            to gamble. I gambled when I went to work in the city. I want to fight
            them on their own ground, not moan about them from a distance. I
            did it and I'm still living. But I've had my fill of these city gutter-
            snipes—all that scavenging scum! They're the sort of people, who,
            if the gates of heaven opened to them, all they'd feel would be a
            draught. I'm wasting away down there. The time has come to act.
            I'm after something truly workable, something deserving of the
            proper and active and voluntary application of my own powers. And
            I'll find it./

{35. S(P) resolves that he must no longer lose time mingling with parasites. Rather one must think one's way out of situations which have not been meaningful or profitable in order to recoup lost time.}

36. LEN: I squashed a tiny insect on a plate the other day. And I brushed the remains off my finger with my thumb. Then I saw that the fragments were growing, like fluff. As they were falling, they were becoming larger, like fluff. I had put my hand into the body of a dead bird./

{36. S(L) talks about having killed an insect only to find that in time his killing hand now dwells inside the body of a dead bird.}

37. PETE: The trouble is, you've got to be quite sure of what you mean by efficient. Look at a nutcracker. You press the cracker and the cracker cracks the nut. You might think that's an exact process. It's not. The nut cracks, but the hinge of the cracker gives out a friction which is completely incidental to the particular idea. It's unnecessary, an escape and wastage of energy to no purpose. So there's nothing efficient about a nutcracker. [PETE *sits, drinks.*]/

{37. S(P) struggles to determine what he means by efficient so that he could recognize it when it occurs.}

38. LEN: They've gone on a picnic.
    MARK: Who?
    LEN: The dwarfs.
    PETE: Oh Christ. [*Picks up paper.*]
    LEN: They've left me to sweep the yard, to keep the place in order. It's a bloody liberty. They're supposed to be keeping you under observation. What do they think I am, a bloody charlady? I can't look after the place by myself, it's not possible. Piles and piles and piles of muck and leavings all over the place, spewed up spewed up, I'm not a skivvy, they don't pay me, I pay them./

{38. S(L) announces that his dwarfs, the assassins, are elsewhere celebrating at a picnic, having already left behind them a previous mess of blood stained feces and other vital fluids that he must now clean up, wondering along the way at whose whim one works, at his or at the dwarfs. Who controls whom? Who bids an assassination? Who cleans up after a murder?}

39. MARK: Why don't you settle down?
    LEN: Oh don't worry, it's basically a happy relationship. I trust them.

They're very efficient. They know what they're waiting for. But they've got a new game, did I tell you? It's to do with beetles and twigs. There's a rockery of red-hot cinder. I like watching them. Their hairs are curled and oily on their necks. Always squatting and bending, dipping their wicks in the custard. Now and again a lick of flame screws up their noses. Do you know what they do? They run wild. They yowl, they pinch, they dribble, they whimper, they gouge, and then they soothe each others' orifices with a local ointment, and then, all gone, all forgotten, they lark about, each with his buddy, get out the nose spray and the scented syringe, settle down for the night with a bun and a doughnut.

PETE: See you Mark. [*Exit.*]/

{39. S(L) declares that his is a happy relationship with the assassin dwarfs in whose world there are efficient projects where one plays, one burns, one invariably defecates into food, arouses and burns the nasal senses, one engages in debauchery, running wild, yowling, pinching, dribbling, whimpering, gouging, soothing each others orifices with ointment, spray on a good scent to conceal the bad smell of the mess, and ultimately settle down and eat. In this domain, then, there is murder, there is confusion between eating and defecating, stimulation, and soothing of bodily orifices.}

40. MARK: Why don't you put it on the table? [*Pause.*] Open it up, Len. [*Pause.*] I'm supposed to be a friend of yours.

LEN: You're a snake in my house.

MARK: Really?

LEN: You're trying to buy and sell me. You think I'm a ventriloquist's dummy. You've got me pinned to the wall before I open my mouth. You've got a tab on me, you're buying me out of house and home you're a calculating bastard. [*Pause.*] Answer me. Say something. [*Pause.*] Do you understand? [*Pause.*) You don't agree? [*Pause.*] You disagree? [*Pause.*] You think I'm mistaken? [*Pause.*] But am I? [*Pause.*] Both of you bastards, you've made a hole in my side, I can't plug it! [*Pause.*] I've lost a kingdom. I suppose you're taking good care of things. Did you know that you and Pete are a musical hall act? What happens? What do you do when you're alone? Do you do a jig? I suppose you're taking good care of things. I've got my treasure too. It's in my corner. Everything's in my corner. Everything is from the corner's point of view. I don't hold the whip. I'm a labouring man. I do the corner's will. I slave my guts out. I thought, at one time, that I'd escaped it, but it never dies, it's never dead. I feed it, it's well fed. Things that at one time seem to me of value I have no resource but to give it to eat and what was of value turns into pus. I can hide nothing. I can't lay anything aside. Nothing can be put aside, nothing can be hidden, nothing can be saved, it waits, it eats, it's voracious, you're in it, Pete's in it, you're all in my corner. There must be somewhere else!

Swift cross fade of lights to down centre area.
PETE is seen vaguely, standing downstage below LEN's *room.* MARK *is seating in his room. Unlit.* LEN *crouches, watching* PETE. /

{40. S(L) perceives that his male friends, S(P) and S(M) treat him as though he were "a ventriloquist's dummy" at their service for their use and feels immobilized, used, all spent and without a domain while the two male colleagues work together. S(L) perceives further that he has a treasure in his corner, a corner that, however, rules him, orders him, enslaves him and never dies; a corner that he has to feed well with what was once of value to him and has changed into pus. For S(L) the world of parasitism, avarice, enslavement, and pus is a wide one and includes all the inhabitants in his circle of friends.}

41.   Pete walks by the river. Under the woodyard wall stops. Stops. Hiss of the yellow grass. The wood battlements jaw over the wall. Dust in the fairground ticks. The night ticks. He hears the tick of the round-about, up river with the sweat. Pete walks by the river. Under the woodyard wall stops. Stops. The wood hangs. Death-mask on the water. pete walks by the—gull. Slicing gull. Gull. Down. He stops. Rat corpse in the yellow grass. Gull pads. Gull probes. Gull stamps his feet. Gull whinnies'up. Gull screams, tears, Pete, tears, digs, pete cuts, breaks, pete stretches the corpse, flaps his wings, Pete's beak grows, probes, digs, pulls, the river jolts, no moon, what can I see, the dwarfs collect, they slide down the bridge, they scutter by the shoreside, the dwarfs collect, capable, industrious, they wear rain-coats, it is going to rain, Pete digs, he screws in to the head, the dwarfs watch, Pete tugs, he tugs, he's tugging, he kills, he's killing, the rat's head, with a snap the cloth of the rat's head tears. pete walks by the... [*Deep groan.*]

He sinks into chair left of his table. Lights in LEN'S *room swiftly fade up.* PETE *turns to him.* /

{41. S(L) experiences his domain as one that includes cannibalism and coprophagia and with the involvement of his friend pete's active killing of animals.}

42. PETE: You look the worse for wear. What's the matter with you?

LEN: I've been ill.

PETE: Ill? What's the matter?

LEN: Cheese. Stale cheese. It got me in the end. I've been eating a lot of cheese.

PETE: Yes, well, it's easy to eat too much cheese.

LEN: It all came out, in about twenty-eight goes. I couldn't stop shivering and I couldn't stop squatting. It got me all right. I'm all right now. I only go three times a day now. I can more or less regulate it. Once in the morning. A quick dash before lunch. Another quick dash after tea, and then I'm free to do what I want. I don't think you understand. That cheese didn't die. It only began to live when you swallowed it, you see, after it had gone down. I bumped into a German one night, he came home with me and helped me finish it off. He took it to bed with him, he sat up in bed with it, in the guest's suite. I went in and had a gander. He had it taped. He was brutal with it. He would bite into it and then concentrate. I had to hand it to him. The sweat came out on his nose but he stayed on his feet. After he'd got out of bed, that was. Stood bolt upright, swallowed it, clicked his fingers, ordered an other piece of black currant pie. It's my pie-making season. His piss stank worse than the cheese. You look in the pink./

{42. S(L) attributes his mental breakdown and subsequent stay in hospital to eating stale cheese, helped as he was by a brutal and voracious German whose urine stank worse than the stale cheese. In this domain even dead, eaten up cheese can relive, inhabit S's (L's) inside and cause debris by turning fluids into smelly and damaging things.}

43. PETE: You want to watch your step. You know that? You're going from bad to worse. Why don't you pull yourself together? Eh? Get a steady job. Cultivate a bit of go and guts for a change. Make yourself useful, mate, for Christ's sake. As you are, you're just a dead weight round everybody's neck. You want to listen to your friends, mate. Who else have you got?

     PETE *taps him on the shoulder and exists. A light comes up on* MARK. *The lights in* LEN'S *room fade out.* LEN *rises to down centre./*

{43. S(P) admonishes S(L) to get a job so that he does not become a burden to him and the other housemate.}

44. LEN: Mark sits by the fireside. Crosses his legs. His fingers wear a ring. The finger poised. Mark regards his finger. He regards his legs. He

regards the fireside. Outside the door is the black blossom. He combs his with an ebony comb, he sits, he lies, he lowers his eye-lashes, raises them, sees no change in the posture of the room, lights a cigarette, watches his hand clasp the lighter, watches the flame, sees his mouth go forward, sees the consummation, is satisfied. Pleased, sees the smoke in the lamp, pleased with the lamp and the smoke and his bulk, pleased with his legs and his ring and his hand and his body in the lamp. Sees himself speaking, the words arranged on his lips, sees himself with pleasure silent.

Under the twigs they slide, by the lilac bush, break the stems, sit, scutter to the edge of the lawn and there wait, capable, industrious, put up their sunshades, watch. Mark lies, heavy, content, watches his smoke in the window, times his puff out, his hand fall, [*with growing disgust*] smiles at absent guests, suck in all corners, arranges his web, lies there a spider.

LEN *moves to above armchair in* MARK'S *room as lights fade up. Down centre area fades out./*

{44. S(L) speaks about S(M) in his presence and describes a scenario where S(M) appears to have a comfortable and sensuous life.}

45.　　What did you say?
　MARK: I never said anything.
　LEN: What do you do when you're tired, go to bed?
　MARK: That's right.
　LEN: You sleep like a log.
　MARK: Yes.
　LEN: What do you do when you wake up?
　MARK: Wake up.
　LEN: I want to ask you a question.
　MARK: No doubt.
　LEN: Are you prepared to answer questions?
　MARK: No.
　LEN: What do you do in the day when you're not walking about?
　MARK: I rest.
　LEN: Where do you find a resting place?
　MARK: Here and there.
　LEN: By consent?
　MARK: Invariably.
　LEN: But you're not particular?
　MARK: Yes, particular.

LEN: You choose your resting place?
MARK: Normally.
LEN: That might be anywhere?
MARK: Yes.
LEN: Does that content you?
MARK: Sure! I've got a home. I know where I live./

{45. S(L) speaks for himself as capable of sleeping a lot, capable of resting anywhere, and knowing how to choose a resting place.}

46. LEN: You mean you've got roots. Why haven't I got roots? My house is older than yours. My family lived here. Why haven't I got a home?
    MARK: Move out./

{46. S(L) shows remorse that he does not have roots and is asked by S(M) to move out.}

47. LEN: Do you believe in God?
    MARK: What?
    LEN: Do you believe in God?
    MARK: Who?
    LEN: God.
    MARK: God?
    LEN: Do you believe in God?
    MARK: Do I believe in God?
    LEN: Yes.
    MARK: Would you say that again?
           LEN *goes swiftly to shelf. Picks up biscuit jar. Offers to* MARK./

{47. S(L) wonders if S(M) believes in God.}

48. LEN: Have a biscuit.
    MARK: Thanks.
    LEN: They're your biscuits.
    MARK: There's two left. Have one yourself.
           LEN *puts biscuits away.*
    LEN: You don't understand. You'll never understand.
    MARK: Really?
    LEN: Do you know what the point is? Do you know what it is?
    MARK: No./

{48. S(L) offers S(M) his own biscuits, feeds S(M) as though the biscuits were his own.}

49. LEN: The point is, who are you? Not why or how, not even what. I can see
what, perhaps, clearly enough. But who are you? It's no use saying
you know who you are just because you tell me you can fit your
particular key into a particular slot, which will only receive your
particular key because that's not foolproof and certainly not conclu-
sive. Just because you're inclined to make these statements of faith
has nothing to do with me. It's not my business. Occasionally I
believe I perceive a little of what you are but that's pure accident.
Pure accident on both our parts, the perceived and the perceiver. It's
nothing like an accident, it's deliberate, it's a joint pretence. We
depend on these accidents, on these contrived accidents, to continue.
It's not important then that it's conspiracy or hallucination./

{49. S(L) insists that who one is is a matter of pure accident created by a joint pretence
between a perceiver and the perceived and in this correspondence the joint pretence
may be either consciously willed or uncannilly wished for, a matter of conspiracy or
one of hallucination.}

50.   What you are, or appear to be to me, or appear to be to you, changes
so quickly, so horrifyingly, I certainly can't keep up with it and I'm
damn sure you can't either. But who you are I can't even begin to
recognize, and sometimes I recognize it so wholly, so forcibly, I can't
look, and how can I be certain of what I see? You have no number.
Where am I to look, where am I to look, what is there to locate, so as to
have some surety, to have some rest from this whole bloody racket?
You're the sum of so many reflections. How many reflections? Whose
reflections?/

{50. For S(L) the contrived accident of perceiver and perceived engage in the joint
venture of creating the stable identity that one has required because the idea of who
one consistently is in some stable form is constantly changing and causes fear for him
and makes him desire some abiding surety from this situation where identity is based
on multiple reflections.}

51.   Is that what you consist of? What scum does the tide leave? What
happens to the scum? When does it happen? I've seen what happens.
But I can't speak when I see it. I can only point a finger. I can't even do
that. The scum is broken and sucked back. I don't see where it goes. I
don't see when, what do I see, what have I seen? What have I seen, the
scum or the essence? What about it? Does all this give you the right to
stand there and tell me you know who you are?/

{51. If the conception of who one is is a potentially fleeting one and no certainty is guaranteed, S(L) suspects that it is impertinent to assume that one really knows anyone. For in conceiving an identity of anyone, one does not know which profile of a person is surface or deep, scum, or essence. }

52.   It's a bloody impertinence. There's a great desert and there's a wind stopping. pete's been eating too much cheese, he's ill from it, it's eating his flesh away, but that doesn't matter, you're still both in the same boat, you're eating all my biscuits, but that doesn't matter, you're still both in the same boat, you're still standing behind the curtains together. He thinks you're a fool, pete thinks you're a fool, but that doesn't matter, you're still both you standing behind my curtains, moving my curtains in my room. He may be your Black Knight, you may be his Black Knight, but I'm cursed with the two of you, with two Black Knight's, that's friendship, that's this that I know. That's what I know.

MARK: Pete thinks I'm a fool? [*Pause.*] Pete... Pete thinks that I'm a fool?

LEN *exits. Lights in* MARK'S *room fade out and then fade in again. Doorbell rings.* MARK *rises, goes off to front door. Silence.* /

{52. S(L) concludes that difficult as it is to be sure of who one is, the identity of one person is potentially interchangeable with that of another. This trap or curse of mutuality and complicit involvement with others is "friendship".}

53. PETE: [*Entering:*] Hullo, Mark.

MARK: [*Re-enters and sits again:*] Hullo.

PETE: What are you doing?

MARK: Nothing.

PETE: Can I sit down?

MARK: Sure.

[PETE *sits right armchair. Pause.*]

PETE: Well, what are you doing with yourself?

MARK: When's that?

PETE: Now.

MARK: Nothing.

MARK *files his nails.*

[*Pause.*]

PETE: LEN's in hospital.

MARK: Len? What's the matter with him?

PETE: Kidney trouble. Not serious. [*Pause.*] Well, what have you been doing with yourself?

MARK: When?

PETE: Since I saw you.

MARK: This and that.
PETE: This and that?
MARK: That.
[*Pause.*]
PETE: Do you want to go and see Len?
MARK: When? Now?
PETE: Yes. It's visiting time. [*Pause.*] Are you busy?
MARK: No. [*Pause.*]
PETE: What's up?
MARK: What?
PETE: What's up?
MARK: What do you mean?
PETE: You're wearing a gasmask.
MARK: Not me.
[*Pause.*]/

{53. S(P) lies to S(M) that S(L) is in hospital with kidney trouble which is not serious and invites S(M) to visit S(L) in hospital with him.}

54. PETE [*Rising:*] Ready?
MARK: Yes. [*He rises and exits.*]
PETE: [*As he follows* MARK *off*] Fine day. [*Pause.*] Bit chilly.
The door slams as they leave the house. Lights up on LEN *in hospital bed. Listening to wireless (earphones).*
PETE *and* MARK *enter.*
LEN: You got here.
PETE: [*Sitting left of bed:*] Yes.
LEN: They can't do anything for me here.
PETE: Why's that?
LEN: Because I'm no trouble. [MARK *sits right of bed.*] They treat me like a king. These nurses, they treat me exactly like a king. [*Pause.*] Mark looks as though he's caught a crab.
MARK: Do I?
PETE: Airy, this ward.
LEN: Best quality blankets, home cooking, everything you could wish for. Look at the ceiling. It's not too high and it's not too low. [*Pause.*]/

{54. S(L) experiences his treatment in hospital as one which makes him think of himself as a king and accordingly he enjoys the air from the space and high ceilings, warm blankets, good home cooking, and all the protection he could wish for.}

55. PETE: By the way, Mark, what happened to your pipe?

MARK: Nothing happened to it.
  [*Pause.*]
LEN: You smoking a pipe? [*Pause.*] What's it like out today?
PETE: Bit chilly.
LEN: Bound to be.
PETE: The sun's come out.
LEN: The sun's come out? [*Pause.*] Well, mark, bring off the treble chance this week?
MARK: Not me.
  [*Pause.*]
LEN: Who's driving the tank?
PETE: What?
LEN: Who's driving the tank?
PETE: Don't ask me. We've been walking up the road back to back.
LEN: You've what? [*Pause.*] You've been walking up the road back to back? [*Pause.*] What are you doing sitting on my bed? You're not supposed to sit on the bed you're supposed to sit on the chairs!
PETE: [*Rising and moving off:*] Well, give me a call when you get out. [*He exits.*]
MARK: [*Rising and following him:*] Well, give me a call. [*He exits.*]
LEN: [*Calling after them:*] How do I know you'll be in?
  Blackout. Lights come up on MARK'S *flat.* MARK *enters and sits.* PETE *enters, glances at* MARK, *sits.* /

{55. Ss (P), (M), and (L) engage in superficial conversation during the hospital visit.}

56. PETE: Horizontal personalities, those places. You're the only vertical. Makes you feel dizzy. [*Pause.*] You ever been inside one of those places?
MARK: I can't remember.
PETE: Right. [*Stubs out cigarette, rises, goes to exit.*]
MARK: All right. Why do you knock on my door?
PETE: What?
MARK: Come on. Why do you knock on my door?
PETE: What are you talking about?
MARK: Why?
PETE: I call to see you.
MARK: What do you want with me? Why come and see me?
PETE: Why?
MARK: You're playing a double game. You've been playing a double game. You've been using me. You've been leading me up the garden.
PETE: Mind how you go.

MARK: You've been wasting my time. For years.
PETE: Don't push me boy.
MARK: You think I'm a fool.
PETE: Is that what I think?
MARK: That's what you think. You think I'm a fool.
PETE: You are a fool.
MARK: You've always thought that.
PETE: From the beginning.
MARK: You've been leading me up the garden.
PETE: And you.
MARK: You know what you are? You're an infection.
PETE: Don't believe it. All I've got to do to destroy you is to leave you as you wish to be.

He walks out of the room. MARK *stares, slowly goes off as lights fade. Lights come up on down centre area. Enter* LEN./

{56. S(M) experiences S(P) as a parasite and an infection. In return S(P) perceives himself as needed by S(M) to survive because in his view, S(M) would perish without him.}

57. LEN: They've stopped eating. It'll be a quick get out when the whistle blows. All their belongings are stacked in piles. They've doused the fire. But I've heard nothing. What is the cause for alarm? Why is everything packed? Why are they ready for the off? But they say nothing. They've cut me off without a penny. And now they've settled down to a wide-eyed kip, crosslegged by the fire. It's insupportable. I'm left in the lurch. Not even a stable frankfurter, a slice of bacon rind, a leaf of cabbage, not even a mouldy piece of salami, like they used to sling me in the days when we told old tales by suntime. They sit, chockfull. But I smell a rat. They seem to be anticipating a rarer dish, a choicer spread. And this change. All about me the change. The yard as I know it is littered with scraps of cat's meat, pig bollocks, tin cans, bird brains, spare parts of all the little animals, a squelching, squealing carpet, all the dwarfs' leavings spittled in the muck, worms stuck in the poisoned ship heaps, the alleys a whirlpool of piss, slime, blood, and fruit juice. Now all is bare. All is clean. All is scrubbed. There is a lawn. There is a shrub. There is a flower./

{57. S(L) experiences a sense of alarm as he notices the readiness of the dwarfs to turn the living dead into carcass. But there is a silence which by itself does not conceal the alarm and anticipation of death. S(L) continues to experience a sense of desolation, starvation, and abandonment. S(L) anticipates that following the death of the living, the carcass will blend in with refuse such as the faeces of the assassins; a blending which in turn creates manured fertile land that in its turn becomes capable of generating a living flower.}

NOTES

1. *The Dwarfs* by Harold Pinter, copyright © 1961, 1966, 1968 by Harold Pinter. Reprinted by permission of Grove/Atlantic, Inc.
2. Given the increase in interest in phenomenological psychological research and in disciplined descriptive research in North America and in Europe, the author would welcome comments and constructive criticism from clinical/research practitioners.

REFERENCES

Apprey, M. (1996). Review of *Sincerity and Other Works: Collected Papers of Donald Meltzer*. Edited by A. Hahn. London: Karnac Books, 1994. *Psychoanal. Books*, 7(2), 168-175.
Giorgi, A.P. (1979). The relation among level, type, and structure and their importance for social science theorizing: A dialogue with Schütz. In: A. Giorgi, R. Knowles, L. Smith (Eds.), *Duquesne Studies in Phenomenology*, vol. 3. Pittsburgh: Duquesne University Press, pp. 81-96.
—— (Ed.) (1985). *Phenomenology and Psychological Research*. Pittsburgh: Duquesne University Press.
Hahn, A. (Ed.) (1994). *Sincerity and Other Works: Collected Papers of Donald Meltzer*. London: Karnac Books.
Kronfeld, A. (1920). *Das Wessen der psychiatrischen erkenntnis*. Berlin: Springer.
Meltzer, D. (1966). The relation of anal masturbation to projective identification. *Int. J. Psycho-Anal.*, 47: 335-342.
—— (1971). Sincerity. In: A. Hahn (Ed.) *Sincerity and Other Works. Collected Papers of Donald Meltzer*. London: Karnac Books, 1994.
—— (1992). *The Claustrum*. Perth: Clunie Press.
Pinter, H. (1959). *The Birthday Party* and *The Room*. New York: Grove Weidenfeld.
—— (1961). *The Dwarfs*. In: Harold Pinter: *Complete Works*, vol. 2. New York: Grove Weidenfeld.
—— (1965). *The Homecoming*. In: Harold Pinter: *Complete Works*, vol. 3. New York: Grove Weidenfeld.
Rustin, M. (1991), *The Good Society and the Inner World: Psychoanalysis, Politics*

and Culture. London and New York: Verso.

Steiner, G. (1975). *After Babel: Aspects of Language and Interpretation.* Oxford: Oxford University Press.

2805 Brookmere Road   JOURNAL OF MELANIE. KLEIN AND OBJECT RELATIONS
Charlottesville, VA 22901   Vol. 15, No. 1, March 1997
USA

REPLY TO MAURICE APPREY'S PAPER

Donald Meltzer

I have been asked (twice) if I would write a response...
It is very gratifying that after the many years in which Kleinian writings
have suffered a virtual ban on teaching in American institutes, a wave of
attention to them has recently arisen. But this has resulted, perhaps inevitably, in a new type of suffering that is possibly more hurtful. I would call it
the typically American take-over bid. This is a fashion that relies on a ghost
vocabulary imported from philosophy. Such, for example, is the threadbare
dialectic derived by Ogden ("The Objects of Psychoanalysis") for the
rewriting of all Kleinian literature. Now Dr. Apprey has invoked George
Steiner's canons of deconstructionist literary criticism to separate the texts
from the authors, leaving everything bloodless—save for a slight injection
of blood at Step 4, called suturing the gap created by "precipitous interpretation."

This apparently scholarly and scientific approach is doubtless all very
well in its own province. However, it quite misses the point of the practice
of Kleinian analysis. Unlike Freudian practice this has developed as an art
form, seeking through truthfulness an approach to the realm of the aesthetic,
perhaps even the spiritual. If it is to be "dubbed esoteric," let it be on this
account rather than on grounds of "precipitous interpretation"—where
"precipitous" is based on the canon that "disciplined description must
precede interpretation." That disciplined *observation* must precede, goes
without saying, if intuitions of transference and countertransference are to
be compared with observations of phenomena. But if one supposes that any
disciplined *description* can do more than touch the surface of what has been
observed, one has not understood the depth and complexity of unconscious
processes nor the limitations of consciousness as an organ of attention.

Unfortunately the above paper demonstrates a confusion in the writer's
mind between words and things. When talking about the confusion between
rectum and vagina, for example, he states that this means one is a "stand-in"
for the other and that this renders "boundaries imprecise," and "elasticity
will prevail." It is not the thing that needs to be precise but the word of

JOURNAL OF MELANIE KLEIN AND OBJECT RELATION, 1997, 15(1), 131-132 reference. This confusion makes it more understandable that Dr. Apprey supposes that by "unpacking Meltzer" and "slowing him down" he can make "a transcendental turn from our findings and broaden our scope so that clinicians who are not psychoanalytically informed can see precisely what we see." We are not painting by numbers and issuing instruction manuals.

23 *Alexandra Road*
Oxford OX2 0DD
England

JOURNAL OF MELANIE KLEIN AND OBJECT RELATIONS
Vol. 15, No. 1, March 1997

REPLY TO DR. APPREY'S PAPER

Meg Harris Williams

Dr. Meltzer has asked me if I would like to add anything to his reply to Dr. Apprey's paper. I suppose it is a type of backhanded compliment for a psychoanalytic paper to receive the same kind of reductive treatment that traditionally psychoanalysts have applied to works of literature in order to systematize them—"eliminating redundancies" (poetic ambiguities), making "sense of the whole" (in a way that poets can't), dividing the text into "a series of meaning units or constituents" of equal size, each then duly "interrogated" and stamped for correctness, and finally "transforming each unit, when relevant, into the language of psychological science." This verbal reconstitution is termed "explicitation" or "description of observable phenomena."

But of course it is not the phenomenon of life or literature which are made "observable" by being "described" in this way: it is the phenomena of the code or canon (deconstruction). If the phenomena don't fit the canon they will be "made redundant." This is intellectual consumerism writ small. Those "theories that appear to be a collection of anomalies" (like those absurd or mysterious complexities of meaning that we find in a poem or a play) can be magically replaced by a nice hygienic "praxis," all in "reader-friendly" language familiar to anyone who has undergone a parallel mental refurbishment ready for entree into "the epistemic conversation of post-modernism." And at last, even Kleinians may be admitted—provided they have undergone the appropriate initiation rites. (So who's afraid of the Claustrum?) But if you find praxicising boring, you can always turn straight to the conclusion (Step 4) for a summary of all you need to know.

It is not surprising that following "pretexts" such as these, the author should assume Meltzer to have used Pinter's plays as a "data base" from which to "precipitate" interpretations. Or that he should then use Meltzer's account as his own "data base" in order to "unpack" him and tidy him away: in short to "explicitate" him. Unfortunately in this "journey from darkness to light" the concepts of *appreciation* and of *learning from* appear to be absent. So does the concept of *discovery*. Dr Meltzer, we remember, speaks of the "fresh ordering of my own thoughts and enrichment of my conceptions" that emerged from his study of Pinter's plays, in addition to the "thousand surprises of unexpected meanings, juxtapositions, and linkages in the works themselves" which came to his attention. He asks the reader to read Pinter's plays for the benefit of their own experience, not in order to burden them with unprecipitated hackwork. Dr. Apprey on the other hand treats the play *The Dwarfs* as unprocessed material waiting to be cut up into byte-size pieces. The result of all this explicitation is that we are served up with a diet that bears little resemblance to the original animal—panfried McNuggets of Meltzer and a congealed Pinter that "won't come out the bottle."

The Bourne   JOURNAL OF MELANIE KLEIN AND OBJECT RELATIONS
Redlands Lane   Vol. 15, No. 1, March 1997
Crondall, Farnham
Surrey GU10 5Rf
England

ILLUSTRATIONS OF PHANTASY AS IMPACTED BY REALITY FACTORS

Robert T. Waska

I am supposing that the mind, in all of its urges and anxieties, is in constant relationship to the external world. In this context, the mind is regularly affecting the environment and this ever reshaped world is then affecting the mind. Phantasy is the cornerstone of this reciprocal bond. It can strengthen and expand pr corrupt and damage the capacities of the ego and the reality principle. Phantasy is an attempt to relationally organize and structure internal and external experiences and is the mind's primary method od struggling toward homeostasis. This paper examines the different reactions patients had to an announced office move. All patients were given four weeks advance notice and told where the new location would be, literally twenty feet next door.

KEY WORDS: Perception; Phantasy; Reality; Intrapsychic; and Transference.

Many papers have explored the idea of phantasy and the theoretical considerations have been enormous. J. Laplanche and J.-B. Pontalis (1973) provide several definitions. Phantasy is an:

Imaginary scene, in which subject is a protagonist, representing... (an unconscious wish) in a manner that is distorted... by defensive processes... (p. 314); ... phantasies do not appear to be reducible to an intentional aim on the part of the desiring object... phantasies are still scripts (*scénarios*) of organized scenes which are capable of dramatization... The subject is invariably present in these scenes... It is not an *object* that the subject imagines and aims at, so to speak, but rather a sequence in which the subject has his own part to play and in which permutations of roles and attributions are possible...; phantasy is also the locus of defensive operations... themselves inseparably bound up with the primary function of phantasy, namely the *mise-en-scène* of desire—a *mise-en-scène* in which what is *prohibited* (*l'interdit*) is always present in the actual formulations of the wish (p. 318).

J. Arlow (1985) states it in this manner:

In the course of treatment one can observe how the symptoms of the patient's illness, how his life history and his love relations, his character structure and his artistic creations may all represent in different ways derivative manifestations of the persistent unconscious fantasy activity, of the "fantasized reality" that governs the individual's life (p. 534).

The *Dictionary of Kleinian Thought* (1991) states:

Phantasy is the mental expression of the instinctual impulses and also of defense mechanisms against instinctual impulses (p. 32).

Finally and most closely linked to the focus of my paper, H. Segal (1974) has written that:

... phantasy forming is a function of the ego. The view of phantasy as a mental expression of instincts through the medium of the ego assumes a higher degree of ego organization then is usually postulated by Freud. It assumes that the ego from birth is capable of forming, and indeed is driven by instincts and anxiety to form primitive object-relationships in phantasy and reality... reality experiences immediately influence and are influenced by unconscious phantasy. Phantasy is not merely an escape from reality, but a constant and unavoidable accompaniment of real experiences, constantly interacting with them... If unconscious phantasy is constantly influencing and altering the perception or interpretation of reality, the converse also holds true: reality impinges on unconscious phantasy (pp. 13-14).

The specific manner in which new data is received and perceived, consciously and unconsciously, provides a crisp window into the inner life of the patient and their particular interface between reality and various intrapsychic phantasy states. The psychoanalytic process involves the understanding of the patient's mind in all of its ramifications; the process of how the self[1] relates to itself and to its objects, via phantasy, is a constant focus of the analytic process.

I conceptualize phantasy as, from the birth of the organism, the foremost and fundamental organizing, binding, and translating energy of the psychic system. In this context, it must be remembered that phantasy states allow for the inner aspects of self and object representations to move and shift in order to defend, battle, and/or adapt to the inner motions of the often opposing and conflictual elements of other constellations of self and object representations. Phantasy allows for inner movement, mutation, and transformation within the matrix of the self and the object representational systems and provides the fuel for this internal motion. In other words, the introjected relationship between the infant and the mother does not remain static, it continues on with a life of its own, constantly being reissued, re-shaped, and recreated by both internal and external reality.

Clinical Material

I will report on various archaic phantasy states in patients as provoked and enhanced by an environmental change, the relocation of my office. After giving all of my patients four weeks notice that I would be moving next door to a new office, I immediately noticed marked transference reactions; these reactions were accompanied by specific phantasies that for many of the patients crystallized upon the actual relocation. I believe this to be the result of the unique impact that reality and phantasy tend to have upon one another; for some patients reality seems to jar away their transference phantasies and for some patients reality seems to fixate the transference phantasies. One reason for this is defensive, in that reality, or at least the illusion of reality, is safer than phantasy for some individuals and for others phantasy is safer than the experience of reality.

For two years, I had been renting an office space in which I shared a waiting room with one other therapist; I then decided to relocate next door, approximately twenty feet away, to a similar office space where I would be the sole practitioner. In the new location, there was one large private office, one large waiting room, a kitchen area, and a bathroom; the floor plan was a mirror image of the old one. I choose to relocate for convenience, the pleasure of having my "own space," and the fact that I didn't particularly enjoy the person with whom I shared the old office. I will present the initial responses or lack of responses of different patients to this new setting; my interest in this was partially fueled by how their reactions seemed to offer a unique view into the intrapsychic mind scape that they usually dwelt in and maneuvered from, as well as a view of the impact of reality factors upon their phantasy material. It was a reinforcement and validation of the theoretical concept of phantasy as a central organizing factor in the mind which has an inseparable relationship to external reality.

Many of my patients noticed the new office setting, looked around a bit, made a comment or two, and then settled in to resume therapy as usual. With this group of patients the majority of the feedback consisted of either comments about how much bigger the space was and how comfortable everything felt or comments about how the floor plan of my office was now reversed and that it was a bit difficult to get used to. These types of superficial or screen comments persisted for a few weeks. On the other hand, there were other patients who had a much more jagged and direct set of responses.

All my patients at the time were being seen one to three times a week in psychoanalytic psychotherapy. I tend to see rather disturbed patients, but I am confident that the ideas I am reporting also apply to the neurotic conflicts of the so called higher functioning patient.

Mr. B looked around the new office very slowly and intently. After a period of time that felt to me like hours, he looked at me blankly. There was no comment. He had taken it in, adjusted himself to it, and looked at me to begin. This data gathering and robot like approach to a new environment was very much the way he usually related to all aspects of life, warding off any hint of affect he might have. This was part of a phantasy in which he protected himself from the "dangerous exposure" he feared would occur if he allowed his feelings to be known.

The next patient was Mr. A. His primary reaction was similar to one of mine in that he was very glad to be rid of the therapist whom I had shared the last suite with. When I saw Mr. A, he often omitted a very loud, out of context, and unusually piercing laughter that persisted for several minutes, at which time the therapist next door would pound on the wall for the noise to stop. I had spoken to the therapist about this and had gotten nowhere except into further unfriendliness. While I had previously asked the patient to quiet down a bit, this was mostly an unfortunate situation in which the other therapist had absolutely no room for any occasional disturbances. At times, his patients would also become loud or obnoxious to the point of intruding upon my work; I have always felt this to be a typical hazard of the work we do and the pitfalls of sharing office space, yet this therapist was unable to discuss it as a mutual concern that could be worked with. The patient and I had mutually agreed that this therapist was therefore selfish and quite insensitive; I had noted a sort of mutual "hate" that grew out of this situation, a hate that seemed to bond us together. These factors were a constant focus within the analysis of the transference and countertransference over the course of the treatment. In the setting of my new office, Mr. A told me he felt a great freedom in being away from the other therapist. It was as though there now was a symbiotic merger state of glee as we mutually celebrated the freedom to express ourselves as we pleased. We were able to explore this as in part symbolic of a freedom that he never had at home with his family and in part symbolic of finally having "someone on his side"; he had been aware of my own feelings of being caught "in the middle" in the old office setting and was glad to have me more available for his own needs. He had grown up in a very oppressive, difficult, and violent atmosphere where it was quite dangerous to express himself. We gradually came to see the piercing laughter as a component of a projective identification process that set the stage for him to be treated as he was in childhood and my office partner banging on the wall was a re-enactment of his early experiences within his family. I was, in the early transference, the ineffectual mother who could do nothing to help protect him from the abusive father; later, in my new office, I was part of his "escape phantasy" where he could rid himself of the noisy father and have a understanding mother all to himself.

Several patients commented that they hoped I would tell them where I was moving to. Upon exploration, they revealed phantasies of coming to their sessions, finding me gone, and not knowing where I had moved to. As we unraveled the transference meanings of this phantasy, the various strands of anxiety concerning abandonment, the fears of separation, and the terror of betrayal came to consciousness. These were patients who had enormous problems regarding phantasies of desiring attachment and dependency followed by terrors of being annihilated as the result of such connections.

Mrs. K had marked negative transference phantasies both before and after I moved. She was convinced that I was moving because I wanted to get rid of her and that since "I was moving up in the world," I would "leave her behind." Feeling that I did not care about her well-being, she hated me for deciding to move. Overall, she felt very unimportant and generally slighted and rejected by me. This made it appear quite easy to make transference interpretations as to her various fears and wishes; unfortunately, with this particular patient making interpretations was like trying to spread frozen butter over a delicate piece of bread. Once I had moved into the new office, she told me that she definitely hated the new environment; she hated everything about it. She shredded each part of my new office into small piles of useless garbage with her criticism. A new light fixture had a rather bright bulb in it and instead of commenting on the brightness, she told me how ugly and offensive it was and how much it damaged her eyes. "You want to burn my eyes out," she cried and yelled. I believe this to be the type of distorted feedback and communication she received from her mother during most of her early years. Agreeing with her realistic observation as to the brightness, I picked out a dimmer bulb for the fixture; by doing this, I was of course also agreeing that I did want to "burn out her eyes" and would now try to undo my attack. When she noticed the change during the next session, she said she was sick and tired of my "techniques" to "break her down." When Mrs. K used this phrase, as she often did, she meant that I must be trying to psychologically trick her, play mental games with her, and generally test her somehow for "secret reasons." She also felt that the change in the bulb would be welcomed by all and therefore it must be a trick on my part to get people to like me more. I asked her why she thought I would work so hard and secretly to have people like me, and if she might be describing her own efforts and hopes for me to like her. I also mentioned to her that there were easier ways to present oneself in a favorable light (so to speak) if one is trying to make connections with people. I suggested that her early experience in life had been very harsh and overpowering and if life's problems receded or dimmed a bit, she might feel unsure and worried. I waited with curiosity for this patient's next volley, as she generously volunteers her ideas on my mode of dress, pattern of speech, choice of office decoration, haircut style, telephone machine message, and whatever else she can find to build her case about how we are too different and will drift apart. Of course, the closer she felt towards me the more intense her terror of abandonment and rejection by me became.

Two female patients made comments to the effect that they would like to move in permanently. "I love it, can I just move right in?" was the way one patient put it. The other woman said, "let us always stay here, we can just sit around and talk all day long and never leave." I commented that she curiously left out what would occur at nightfall.

One patient has not shown up for appointments since I moved. I had a feeling that the move was, in phantasy, a perceived re-enactment of total abandonment which she had felt constantly in her early years, causing her to flee from me in fear of annihilation, a sort of "I will get him before he gets me" type of situation may have occurred. She has never returned my calls.

Another patient, Mrs. M, had a very immediate reaction the first time she came into the new office. She told me that she had realized it before, but now that she saw this new office she had proof that I was merely out to make money. She said that I was robbing people and only seeking my own pleasure and the new office furniture was proof of this idea. This woman is usually in a state of fluctuation between projecting a rejecting internal object into me and projecting a rewarding or exciting object into me. I gently reminded Mrs. M that I actually was seeing her for a reduced fee and that I could not make a profit off of her if I wanted to, given that she is not even paying my lowest fee. I also made a genetic transference interpretation concerning her feeling ripped off and taken advantage of from me, as similar to her experience in her family where she felt worthless and was only alive to be taken advantage of. We gradually were able to explore her use of this accusatory method of relating as a way of protecting her from the fears she had of my not having any interest, care, or love for her. This would be an example of a clarification of reality followed by a genetic interpretation paving the way to the more "here and now" transference phantasy material;

it is often just as true that a comment about the current transference matrix will pave the way to genetic material. It does seem that each patient's response to one or the other line of investigation is dependent on the vicissitudes of their internal phantasy world and the resulting psychological matrix that colors their relationships with the analyst and others in their life.

One patient, who is usually very timid, was fearful and shy about the idea of a new office. She had a hard time coming into the waiting room and was very afraid that she was disturbing me and so I had to coax her into the room assuring her that she was welcome and was certainly not disturbing me. This woman had an enduring childhood phantasy in which she was always causing trouble and disturbing people.

I hope to be illustrating how easily these patient's primary phantasy configurations came alive in the context of an environmental change. While many of my examples are of rather gross behavior with very regressed patients, I believe the concept of environmental stimuli that is relatively innocuous on a manifest level being the trigger for archaic phantasy productions is applicable to more neurotic patients as well.

One patient who had been the subject of his father's sadistic emotional attacks for years, wherein his own identity seemed to be stolen from him over and over, remarked that the door to my waiting room was unlocked. I told him "Yes, it is open for patients like yourself to come in and sit down until I come out for you." He replied "Any kleptomaniac that was walking by could come in and clean you out." This is a man who feels the world is impinging upon him and that people usually have evil motives and frequently take advantage of each other, taking away emotional bits and pieces as they wish. The internal object representations of his father were often of a sadistic and psychotic nature and these as well as his own wishes were always very warded off and usually projected outwards as greed, lust, and violence coming from threatening strangers. I asked him if there was anything he was interested in the waiting room. This started what proved to be a fruitful session about his own desires, or rather his seemly lack of desires and wishes.

One patient who is loyal to the interest of placating, rescuing, and caretaking others at any cost was walking around outside, waiting for me to open the new office. It was her first time in it and I was running five minutes late. I noticed that she was pacing around furiously. Not until late into the session was she able to say that indeed she was furious that I was late but felt it was not "proper" to show her anger because it was "my day," meaning my first day in my new office and she didn't want to "spoil it." Instead, she praised me for the new office setting and held off expressing her rage. I pointed out that this was a very common theme in her life, where in she sacrificed herself for the sake of others through some sort of rationalization which in the long run created a pathological relationship very similar to the one she had with her mother. She was sure I was celebrating and basking in my own glory and didn't want to be bothered with the needs of anyone else. Indeed, we eventually discussed the fear and excitement concerning her "first day" in my new office that was being projected into myself and then defended against. We explored how distant we were to each other in this particular phantasy, leaving her alone and unable to reach me for help or closeness.

Some patients did not appear to realize the office change. No comment was made and they did not even look around at anything. Months, and now years, later they still have not given any indication that they are consciously aware of the change. I speculate that this is a remarkable demonstration of the total autistic encapsulation that they have constructed within parts of their psyche for a state of total yet paradoxical protection. These are patients who appear to be deadened and often have phantasies about the need to remain buried safely behind a protective shield from the overwhelming and destructive qualities of the world at large and intimacy with the analyst in particular.

Summary

I hope this short paper points out the various ways patients' transference and phantasy processes are constantly in motion and how these phantasies are constantly shaped by reality factors. Mental functions, including phantasy, are woven into and around all internal and external factors; this allows the analyst many chances to gather information as to the exact nature of the patient's psychic structure and the accompanying phantasy elements. The analyst is then in a position to make usable interpretations and begin to unravel the phantasy material in the context of the clinical transference and the projective identification processes that are ubiquitous to the analytic relationship.

NOTE

1. The infant begins life with all of its various neurological states of flux, psychological and physical tensions, somatic and cognitive experiences, and multiple complex interfaces with environmental stimuli. From the very start the infantile organism seeks out the object and the phantasy of the object in order to bring about a subjective sense of organization, discharge, and understanding, at first in more primitive ways and later with more sophisti-

cated expression and intent. These potentials of mind and body are innate and, in combination, make up the emerging substrate's of the self. The developing and never static nature of the self exists in part as the combination of the psychological and biological needs and functions of the human organism including the multiple aspects of somatic states, core affects, mental wishes, and fears of both a predatory and a persecutory nature, united with all of the varied integrative and perceptual aspects and psychic components of the Ego, such as self and object representations, and compromise formations. These organizing functions of the human organism in addition to the subjective experience of one's self as a person and a body, the experience of being both passive and active, and the sense of being both an individual "one" and of being part of a whole are all fundamentally shaped, organized, and translated by unconscious phantasy to produce what is understood as the Self. This end product of phantasy formation remains the central fulcrum from which all future experiences revolve in some manner or form.

REFERENCES

Arlow, J. (1985). The concept of psychic reality and related problems. *J. Amer. Psychoanal. Assn.*, 33: 521-535.
Hinshelwood, R.D. (1991). *A Dictionary of Kleinian Thought*. Northvale, NJ: Jason Aronson.
Laplanche, J., Pontalis, J.-B. (1973). *The Language of Psychoanalysis*. New York: Norton.
Segal, H. (1974). *An Introduction to the Work of Melanie Klein*. New York: Basic Books.

P.O. 2769   **Journal of Melanie Klein and Object Relations**
San Anselmo, CA, 94979   Vol. 15, No. 1, March 1997
USA

COUNTERTRANSFERENCE AND DISABILITY:
SOME OBSERVATIONS

Kenneth R. Thomas

The purpose of this paper is to identify and discuss the types of countertransference reactions that analysts and other therapists might be expected to have toward patients with physical disabilities. A brief history of the problems and uses of countertransference is presented and examples of common countertransference problems in treating patients with disabilities are provided. Among the psychodynamic factors likely to evoke countertransference reactions are castration anxiety, fear of loss of love, fear of loss of the object, fear of death, anxiety regarding self disintegration, and selected ego defense mechanisms such as projection, denial, and restriction of the ego. Therapists are urged not to condemn themselves for having such reactions but to use their reactions to gain insight into the present characteristics of the transference relationship and psychological status of their patients.

KEY WORDS: Countertransference; Disability; Freud; Racker; Castration Anxiety; Loss; and Defense Mechanisms.

The literature is replete with studies in which the attitudes of others toward people with physical disabilities have been investigated (e.g., see Yuker, 1988). In fact, a survey by Berven (1991) indicated that approximately 20% of studies published recently in *Rehabilitation Psychology* addressed the issue of attitudes toward people with disabilities. Although a comprehensive summary of the results and implications of these studies is beyond the scope of this paper, it is clear that the presence of a physical disability may affect, often in negative, but sometimes in positive ways, the reactions of others.

In the psychoanalytic literature, the most comprehensive discussion of these issues was presented by Siller (1988). Although Siller subscribed wholeheartedly to Cowen, Underberg, and Verillo's (1958) notion that attitudes toward persons with disabilities are, "... multiply caused... (by) psychodynamic, situational, sociocultural, and historical developments..."

(p. 303), he argued strongly for the recognition of intrapsychic phenomena. Specifically noted as phenomena deserving further recognition and research were psychoanalytic concepts such as self representation, quality of object relationship, anaclitic and narcissistic object choices, and ego defenses. In addition, the research literature on the relationships between attitudes toward disability and "abstract" psychoanalytic concepts such as castration anxiety, body ego, identification, body ego boundaries, and ego strength was reviewed. Summarizing a position that he had taken in an earlier paper, Siller (1984) observed that "... To say that a flexible defense style or low castration anxiety or more mature object representation are associated with acceptance of the disabled does not reduce the attitude phenomenon to those personality characteristics. Rather, it suggests that such persons are better able to cope with potential stress emanating from the discrimination of a deviant physical state..." (p. 221). Siller's remarks relate not only to the everyday reactions of non-clinicians toward persons with disabilities, but also to the countertransference reactions of therapists toward their patients who are physically disabled or have serious physical illnesses.

Also important in terms of identifying potential areas of countertransference in treating patients with physical disabilities is the research literature on verbal interactions. Considered collectively, early research in this area (e.g., Barker, Wright, Meyerson, and Gonick, 1953; Kleck, 1968; Kleck, Ono, and Hastorf, 1966) suggested that when interacting with persons with disabilities, persons without disabilities tend to complete the interaction sooner, be agreeable, be less variable in their verbal behavior, and overcompensate in their favorable impressions. To facilitate more "normal" or comfortable interactions, Glasser and Strauss (1964) recommended that both parties in the interaction pretend not to "zero in" on the disability; that is, both parties were encouraged to perceive that he or she was interacting with another *person* rather than focusing on the disability. More recently, Fichten and Amsel (1988) recommended that efforts intended to make interactions more comfortable should concentrate on changing the person without a disability's cognitions about the person with a disability.

Pursuing a line of thought that began over 20 years ago Britton and Thomas (1972), Huebner and Thomas (1995), Lynch and Thomas (1994), Thomas and Garske (1995), and Thomas (1995) have argued that attitudes toward persons with disabilities and interactions with such persons are the result of an interactive process. That is, persons with disabilities are neither the helpless victims of negative attitudes, nor the passive recipients of friendly or hostile interactions; rather, they can significantly affect attitudes and interactions with their own behavior.

Two papers written recently that serve to illustrate the importance of these ideas for psychoanalytic theory and practice are Huebner and Thomas (1995) and Thomas and Garske (1995). Huebner and Thomas (1995) argued that the three major aspects of attachment behavior in human beings (i.e., neurological influences, interpersonal and intrapersonal factors, and social factors) are not only reciprocally interactive, but are also complicated by the presence of childhood disability. That is, the presence of a disability may affect not only the attachment behavior of one's parents, but also, in turn, the personality structure of the person with a disability. Drawing on the theoretical basis offered by Melanie Klein, W.R.D. Fairbairn, and D.W. Winnicott, Thomas and Garske (1995) suggested that these early parent-child interactions could be analyzed and then used to direct both rehabilitation and psychotherapeutic treatment programs. An explicit assumption in both the Huebner and Thomas (1995) and Thomas and Garske (1995) papers was the idea that the infant with a disability may elicit rather unique reactions on the part of his or her parents, which may have significant implications for the infant's later psychological adjustment. The evidence is compelling, for example, that children with physical disabilities are significantly more likely to develop emotional problems than other children (Breslau, 1985; Cadman, Boyle, Szatmari, and Offord, 1987; Rutter, 1981; Siedel, Chadwick, and Rutter, 1975), and adults with disabilities are more likely to experience anxiety and depression than other adults (Turner and McLean, 1989).

Although one might expect that therapists, especially therapists who have been analyzed or experienced some other form of long term counseling or psychotherapy, would have less difficulty than others in reacting objectively to clients with disabilities, no individual, regardless of how psychologically healthy or how long he or she has been in therapy, is immune to socio-cultural biases or unconscious fears of castration, loss of love, or disintegration of the self. Moreover, as pointed out by Thomas and McGinnis (1991), persons with severe cognitive or emotional problems are bound to give helpers many *objective* reasons to both love and hate them. In other words, therapists treating patients with disabilities could be expected to have, not only the usual gamut of counter-transferential responses (e.g., oedipal love, hate or envy), but also a range of responses related to the disability itself.

The purpose of the present paper is to identify and discuss some of the major countertransferential reactions that therapists might have toward their patients with physical disabilities. Although the focus of the paper is on countertransference reactions to patients with physical disabilities, many of these same reactions may be observed in reactions to patients who have cognitive or behavioral deficits or who are physically ill. Also discussed are some techniques therapists can employ to use these reactions to understand and help their patients.

Countertransference: A Brief History

Formal debate on the problem of countertransference began with the publication of Freud's classic article on "The Future Prospects of Psycho-Analytic Therapy" (1910). The first recorded case of countertransference in a psychotherapeutic situation occurred during Josef Breuer's treatment of Anna O. (Breuer and Freud, 1893-1895). As is evident to any sensitive reader of Breuer's presentation of the case, his description of Anna O. in the introduction of the case material reflects affects that are hardly entirely objective (i.e., his observations could easily be interpreted as providing a description of his lover instead of his patient). In the end, Breuer was so disturbed at the sexual transference that Anna developed toward him (e.g., she had hysterical symptoms of pregnancy and childbirth) that he terminated the treatment prematurely and took a "romantic" vacation with his wife, which apparently resulted in his wife becoming pregnant (Jones, 1953). In short, Breuer was unable to "contain" and later use his countertransference reactions to understand and treat Anna. Instead, he became frightened and fled the field.

The status of countertransference as a phenomenon associated with the offering of counseling or psychotherapy has changed markedly over the years. Freud's view (1910), which predominated until the 1950s, was that countertransference "... arises in him (the physician) as a result of the patient's influence on his unconscious feelings, and we are almost inclined to insist that he shall recognize this counter-transference in himself and overcome it" (pp. 144-145). Freud also believed that "... no psycho-analyst goes further than his own complexes and internal resistances permit" (p. 145). To overcome this countertransference, Freud recommended that the physician "... shall begin his activity with a self- analysis and continually carry it deeper while he is making his observations on his patients. Anyone who fails to produce results in a self-analysis of this kind may at once give up any idea of being able to treat patients by analysis" (p. 145). In other words, Freud regarded countertransference as something that the therapist should analyze and overcome. Despite these warnings, Freud wrote only two years later in one of his "technique" papers that the analyst "... must turn his own unconscious like a receptive organ toward the transmitting unconscious of the patient" (p. 115). According to Epstein and Feiner (1979), these two thematic constructs, countertransference as a hindrance, and the analyst's use of his or her own unconscious to understand the patient, have intertwined throughout the historical development of psychoanalytic treatment.

Although the topic of countertransference or, more generally, the analyst's response to the patient was addressed in several important psychoanalytic papers following Freud's introduction of the topic (e.g., Balint and Balint, 1939; Ferenczi and Rank, 1923; Horney, 1939; Reich, W., 1933), it was not until the 1940s and 50s that a new approach to countertransference developed (Epstein and Feiner, 1979; Wolstein, 1988). According to Epstein and Feiner (1979), the most significant contributors to the idea that countertransference was somewhat more than a hindrance to psychoanalytic progress were Heimann (1950, 1960), Little (1951, 1957, 1960), Winnicott (1949, 1960), and Racker (1953, 1957, 1968). In marked contrast to the traditional view, Heimann (1950) declared "the analyst's emotional response to his patient... (is) one of the most important tools for his work" (p. 81). Heimann did not believe, however, that the analyst's response should be communicated to the patient; rather, it should be used as a source of insight into the patient's conflicts and defenses (Epstein and Feiner, 1979). Little (1951, 1957, 1960) shared Heimann's enthusiasm for the importance of the analyst's responses to the patient. In fact, she believed that with severely disturbed patients especially, the analyst's countertransference responses were the most important aspect of the treatment. Among her more startling recommendations was the idea that analysts must feel free to react, sometimes even spontaneously and primitively to their patients, since it is only with their analyst that some patients are able to have genuine human contact.

Winnicott (1949, 1960) wrote two widely cited papers on countertransference. In the first paper, he distinguished between idiosyncratic and therapeutically useful countertransference, and discussed the importance of objective hate in the countertransference, which he felt was necessary for some patients to evoke as part of a natural maturational process. The potential relevance of this concept for treating patients with disabilities was alluded to above. In the second paper, Winnicott recommended that the term countertransference be used only to refer to "that which we hope to eliminate by selection and analysis and the training of analysts... (which) would leave us free to discuss the many interesting things analysts can do with psychotic patients who are temporarily regressed and dependent for which we could use Margaret Little's term: the analyst's total response to the patient's needs" (p. 21).

Although acknowledging other major contributors to the "modern" psychoanalytic literature on countertransference (e.g., Cohen, 1952; Gill,

1983; Gitelson, 1952; Grinberg, 1962; Langs, 1976; Orr, 1955; Reich, A., 1951, 1960, 1966; Sandler, 1976; Searles, 1959, 1967; Stone, 1961; Tauber, 1954; Thompson, 1956; Tower, 1956; Wolstein, 1983), no discussion of counter-transference would be complete without a detailed presentation of Heinrich Racker's contributions (1968). More than any other author Racker provided an intensive analysis of the meanings and uses of countertransference. Racker believed that countertransference, like transference, can be assigned three meanings: (1) It may be a great danger; (2) It can be an important tool for understanding, an assistance to the analyst in his (her) functioning as an interpreter; and (3) It affects the analyst's behavior (i.e., it interferes with the analyst's action as an object of the patient's re-experience in the analytic situation). In addition, he believed that the paucity of scientific investigation about countertransference was due primarily to a rejection by analysts of their own countertransferences. Moreover, like Searles (1959), he believed that the analyst's failure to accept countertransference at least partially explains why the Oedipus complex of the child toward its parents and the patient toward the analyst (transference) has been so much more fully considered than that of the parents toward their children and analysts toward their patients.

Racker was also noted for pointing out that analysis was not an interaction between a "sick" person and a "healthy" person but rather an interaction between two personalities, and he maintained that true objectivity in analysis is based on the analyst's ability to make his or her own subjectivity and countertransference the object of continuous observation and analysis. He distinguished between two types of analyst identifications with the patient: concordant identifications (e.g., the analyst's id with the patient's id) and complementary identifications (e.g., the analyst's ego with the patient's superego). Concordant identifications are based on introjection and projection and complementary identifications are produced by the fact that the patient treats the analyst as an internal (projected) object, and in consequence, the analyst feels treated as such and identifies with this object. Although it is still common practice, Racker believed it was a mistake to apply the term "countertransference" only to complementary identifications.

Another important aspect of Racker's work was the idea that every transference situation provokes a countertransference situation, which arises out of the analyst's identification of him or herself with the patient's (internal) objects (i.e., the complementary countertransference). These countertransference reactions are governed especially by the *law of talion;* thus, every positive transference is answered by a positive countertransference and every negative transference by a negative countertransference. According to Racker, the only way to break the "vicious circle" set in motion by this law is for the analyst to interpret rather than be ruled by the reactions.

Racker also distinguished between two types of countertransference responses. The first type he called countertransference thoughts and the second countertransference positions. The critical difference between these two responses is the degree to which the analyst's ego is involved. In the first type, which arises from the existence of an "analogous situation," the reactions are experienced as thoughts, free associations, or fantasies, with no great emotional intensity. In the second type, which results from an "acting out" on the part of the patient, the analyst's ego is involved and the experience is felt as being true reality. Whether the analyst responds to these situations by perceiving or acting out depends largely on the analyst's own neurosis, inclination to anxiety, defense mechanisms, and inclination to repeat instead of making conscious. Finally, at least for the purposes of the present paper, Racker identified and discussed the implications of different types of countertransference reactions such as anxiety, aggression, guilt feelings, and boredom or somnolence.

A more recent and particularly useful perspective is that countertransference, broadly conceptualized as a manifestation of the analyst's psychological structures and organizing activity, has a decisive effect in determining the nature of the transference (Stolorow, Brandchaft, and Atwood, 1987). From this perspective, which has been labeled an intersubjective approach, transference and countertransference form an intersubjective system of reciprocal mutual influence. Importantly, in using this approach, the reality of the patient's perceptions is never debated nor confirmed; rather, these perceptions serve as points of departure for an exploration of the meanings and organizing principles that structure the patient's psychic reality.

A major assumption of the present paper is that all therapists, whether analysts or not, are subject to and can use their countertransference responses to understand and help their patients. Moreover, it is assumed that the therapist's reactions to disability will affect the quality and nature of the transference and other important aspects of the therapeutic relationship. Finally, it is assumed that patients with physical disabilities, largely because of the close developmental connection between the body and the ego, will tend to evoke specific types of countertransference responses from their therapists. In the presentation that follows an attempt will be made to identify those areas where therapists might expect to experience conscious or unconscious reactions to their patients with disabilities and to demonstrate how these reactions can be used to improve psychotherapeutic outcome and to help the patients better understand themselves.

Common Countertransference Reactions

Cubbage and Thomas (1989) recently delineated the close relationship between what Freud had written generally and the psychology of disability. Prominent among the relevant, classical psychoanalytic concepts was the idea of castration anxiety, which as pointed out by Siller (1988), has been investigated in several studies as a correlate of attitudes toward disability. The term "castration anxiety," as used in classical psychoanalytic theory, can refer to a specific developmental period (i.e., the oedipal period) or to a type of anxiety associated with psychopathology. According to Giovacchini (1982), Freud used the term castration anxiety quite broadly; that is, he considered *any separation* from the body to represent castration, even the loss of feces, which is experienced regressively as castration anxiety. In his writings, Freud related two specific types of disability, blindness (1924a) and amputation (1933), to symbolic castration; however, the concept of castration anxiety is useful for understanding unconscious reactions to virtually all types of disabilities, especially physical disabilities. The logic behind this association may be stated simply as follows: To the person with a disability, the disability may represent a form of castration; to the person without a disability, the sight of a person with a disability may evoke the threat of castration. If it may be assumed that conscious or unconscious fears about castration (or more generally fears about one's body being hurt or damaged) are present in all humans, then it may be inferred that the condition of disability in one's patients could easily trigger a countertransference response in the therapist.

When confronted with such feelings therapists may experience a variety of reactions, including "imaginary" pangs of pain in the genital area, headaches, dizziness, or other physical symptoms, or they may find their free associations turning to thoughts about their parents or their own physical health or safety. Instead of rejecting these reactions or condemning themselves for having these reactions, therapists can use their responses to generate hypotheses about what the patient may be feeling about the loss of body integrity or the vulnerability that the patient may be feeling in relation to the therapist. Whether these feelings are actually communicated to the patient will necessarily depend on the patient's emotional maturity and/or readiness to consider or accept interpretations of this type, but the information itself may be crucial for understanding the patient's present psychological status or the status of the transference.

A related concept, also derived from classical psychoanalytic theory, is "fear of loss of love." Although typically associated more with women than with men because of the Freudian idea that women feel inferior after they have discovered the absence of a penis (1924b), an unconscious (or conscious) fear of loss of love due to the onset or presence of a disability can, like castration anxiety, apply to members of both genders. Moreover, these feelings can exist, not only in patients with disabilities, but also as countertransference reactions in therapists who are treating such patients. Therapist feelings of rejection, loss, or depression when treating patients with disabilities may suggest that the therapist has identified with the patient and that the therapist's reactions are accurately mirroring what the patient is feeling. The therapist's reactions may also, of course, reflect incompletely analyzed aspects of the therapist's own personality, or they may relate more to the patient's unconscious assessment of the therapist's views toward the patient than to issues related to the presence of a disability per se. However, regardless of their origin, the affects evoking these reactions will need eventually to be recognized and addressed by both of the parties in the interaction.

The concept of "fear of the loss of the object" (Freud, 1926) is also relevant here, especially because in the case of many disabilities, a limb or significant physical or mental function has, indeed, been lost. Again, the therapist may sense a feeling of loss or depression, or may find her/himself actively defending against such feelings through associations of power or belongingness (e.g., thinking about his/her superiority to the client or about cherished family members and friends). The concept of fear of the loss of the object is, of course, closely related to the process of mourning, which according to Freud (1917) involves a loss of the object, a loss of interest in the outside world, a cessation of activity, and a loss of capacity to adopt a new love object. Also relevant are Freud's (1914) comments regarding the reactions of persons suffering organic pain and discomfort. Specifically, such persons relinquish their interest in the outside world and withdraw libido from their love objects. All of these reactions have been associated with the onset of disability and all have the potential to evoke concordant or complementary countertransference reactions from the therapist.

Patients with disabilities may also evoke an unconscious fear of death in their therapists. Livneh (1985), for example, found a strong correlation between a person's fear of death and negative attitudes toward people with disabilities. Therapists, perhaps especially those in medical settings, are hardly immune to such unconscious fears and are likely to defend against them in ways that inhibit an open expression of feelings. Similar reactions may be observed in the inordinately happy, upbeat atmosphere that often characterizes hospital visits with a critically ill friend or relative. Unfortunately, although such a stance on the part of the therapist may facilitate the replacement of negative thoughts with positive thoughts, the patient is never permitted the opportunity to express, validate, and work through what are perfectly valid associations between death and disability. That is, the patient is not permitted the opportunity to mourn the loss of an object or function that has unconsciously been associated with life. As stated by Cubbage and Thomas (1989), "Mourning consists of reality testing, a realization that loss truly exists" (p. 169). If the purpose of therapy is to encourage patients to express their feelings or help to make the unconscious conscious, then therapists must be willing to discuss virtually any topic that they sense is important to the patient. It is, in fact, the therapist's willingness to recognize, accept and discuss unpleasant affects, strivings, and fears that makes the therapist a therapist and facilitates personality integration on the part of the patient.

According to Cook (1992), the conceptualization of the ego defenses is the strongest contribution offered by psychoanalysis to the study and understanding of adjustment to disability. The four most prominent defense mechanisms listed by Cook in this regard were repression, projection, reaction formation, and regression. To this list, Cubbage and Thomas (1989) added denial, compensation, displacement, sublimation, restriction of the ego, and rationalization. The use of none of these defense mechanisms is, of course, limited to persons with disabilities. However, the therapist treating patients with disabilities needs to be especially sensitive to the effects that the patient's use of projection, denial, restriction of the ego, and displacement may have on the therapist and on the treatment generally. For example, the patient may project onto the therapist punitive characteristics of the patient's own superego and then act in ways that evoke similar types of countertransference reactions from the therapist. These situations are frequently seen in rehabilitation settings when patients fail to comply with jointly-decided-upon rehabilitation plans and then blame the therapist for being too demanding or for endorsing an inappropriate plan. The therapist's first reaction may be to scold the patient or to absolve, in a parent like fashion, the patient of blame. A better idea would be for the therapist to make note of his or her affective reactions to the situation and then use these reactions to help the patient understand the intrapsychic factors involved.

Perhaps the most frequently seen defense mechanism in rehabilitation settings is denial, especially during the early stages of treatment. In fact, according to several rehabilitation scholars, denial of long-term disability during the early phase of rehabilitation can be a valid, useful, and healthy defense (Gwyther, 1984; Krueger, 1981-1982; Trieschmann, 1981, 1988; Tucker, 1984). Krueger (1981-1982), for example, observed that "... denial may incorporate the initial useful stance of maintaining that recovery will be vigorous and complete. Denial is a necessary defense mechanism, since it is beyond the capacity of most individuals to easily accept such a sudden drastic change in their self concept" (p. 184). Because denial can serve a useful psychological purpose insofar as it helps the patient to cope with the disability, therapists need to be very careful in how they let their own reactions affect the treatment situation. It may, for example, be inappropriate to interpret or otherwise make the patient aware of the denial, even though the therapist has sensed from his or her own concordant countertransference responses that denial is taking place. On the other hand, since a persistent denial of the long-term effects of a disability can be both psychologically and physically dangerous, therapists must be aware that their own fears about disablement may cause them to reinforce the denial, either through reassurance or by failing to address the patient's legitimate (but denied) concerns about the impact of the disability.

One of the more common defense mechanisms used by persons with disabilities is restriction of the ego. In ego restriction disagreeable external impressions in the present are warded off because they might result in the revival of similar impressions from the past (Freud, A., 1936, p. 101). For example, the sight of another person's superior achievement in an area where the person with a disability was once superior may symbolize (unconsciously) the sight of larger genitals, which may evoke the hopelessness of earlier oedipal or sibling rivalries. As a result, the individual avoids any discussion of activities where there is risk of failure or humiliation. Some typical countertransference responses to the use of this defense mechanism might include feelings of wanting to change the topic, boredom, or somnolence.

In the case of displacement, the primary concern of the therapists will be to use their psychoanalytic training and countertransference reactions to analyze what· is really occurring in the psychoanalytic relationship. For example, feelings of being attacked when the patient is criticizing a colleague may signify a negative transference situation, or unexpected feelings of profound love for the patient may signify that the patient is experiencing a break in empathy from the therapist or rejection by a significant other.

In a recent paper comparing how drive theorists and self psychologists might treat a fictitious analysand with an adventitious disability (Thomas, 1994), it was argued that the psychoanalytic stance advocated by Kohut (1959, 1979, 1982), with its emphasis on empathy and the bolstering of self esteem, could offer some significant clinical advantages in the treatment of patients with disabilities. The rationale behind this conclusion was that a disability, if cognitively appraised, could represent a narcissistic insult which would lead to feelings of diminishment, which could in turn lead to lowered self esteem, feelings of shame, and anxiety regarding self disintegration. Although Kohut would typically classify reactions to a physical disability as belonging to what he labeled *a secondary disturbance of the self* (i.e., the reaction of a structurally unimpaired self to the vicissitudes of life), as opposed to *a primary disturbance of the self* such as a psychosis, borderline state, or narcissistic behavior or personality disorder (Kohut and Wolf, 1978, p. 415), the types of transference and countertransference reactions in the treatment situation could be quite similar. For example, a person recently disabled could easily require a mirroring selfobject to confirm his or her innate sense of vigor, greatness, and perfection and/or an idealized parent imago to whom the person could look up to and with whom the person could merge as an image of calmness, infallibility, and omnipotence (Kohut and Wolf, 1978, p. 414). In fact, one frequently sees similar reactions when persons place their trust in God, a physician, or some other authority in response to a life-threatening situation or other serious calamity. In other words, the patient with a disability, regardless of whether a primary disorder of the self is present, may develop a mirroring and/or idealizing transference with the therapist, which the therapist will need to respond to empathically if growth is to occur.

Unfortunately, because the sight or thought of the patient's disability may also evoke defensive reactions against fears of self disintegration on the part of the therapist, it may be difficult for the therapist to perform the necessary selfobject functions. Evidence that such reactions are present could be provided by the therapist finding him or herself making unrealistic assessments about the patient's incredible bravery in the face of adversity or experiencing feelings of guilt about being physically intact (i.e., assuming that the therapist is physically intact). Such feelings could signal disruptions in the therapist's own self structure, a break in empathy in the treatment situation, or simply a need for the therapist to direct his or her efforts toward providing more developmentally appropriate selfobject functions.

Conclusion

Although therapists who are treating patients with disabilities may expect to experience the full gamut of countertransference reactions, the close developmental relationship between the ego (or self) and the body suggests that certain types of reactions will predominate. Among these are reactions that are linked unconsciously to castration anxiety, fear of loss of love, fear of loss of the object, fear of death, fear of self disintegration, and defense mechanisms such as denial, projection and restriction of the ego. In addition to these psychodynamic responses, therapists may expect to experience many of the same situational, socio-cultural, and historical reactions to disability as other persons. The purpose of this paper was not to condemn therapists for having these countertransference reactions, but rather to demonstrate how therapists might use these reactions to better understand and interpret the treatment situation and psychodynamic status of their patients with disabilities.

REFERENCES

Balint, A., Balint, M. (1939). On transference and countertransference. *Int. J. Psycho-Anal.*, 20: 223-230.
Barker, R.G., Wright, B.A., Meyerson, L., Gonick, M.R. (1953). *Adjustment to Physical Handicap and Illness: A Survey of the Social Psychology of Physique and Disability* (Rev. ed.). New York: Social Science Research Council.
Berven, N.L. (1991). Introduction: Attitudes toward people with disabilities. In: M.G. Eisenberg and R.L. Glueckauf (Eds.), *Empirical Approaches to the Psychological Aspects of Disabilities*. New York: Springer, pp. 3-5.
Breslau, N. (1985). Psychiatric disorder in children with physical disabilities. *J. Amer. Acad. Child Psychia.*, 24: 87-94.
Breuer, J., Freud, S. (1893-1895). *S. E.*, 2, 1955, pp. 1-311. In: J. Strachey (Ed.), *The Standard Edition of the Complete Psychological Works of Sigmund Freud*. London: Hogarth Press and The Institute of Psycho-Analysis, 1953-1974.
Britton, J.O., Thomas, K.R. (1972). Modifying attitudes toward the disabled: An interactive approach. *Amer. Arch. Rehab. Ther.*, 20: 112-114.
Cadman, D., Boyle, M., Szatmari, P., Offord, D.R. (1987). Chronic illness, disability, and mental and social well-being: Findings of the Ontario child health study. *Pediatrics*, 79: 805-813.
Cohen, M.B. (1952). Countertransference and anxiety. *Psychia.*, 15: 231-243.
Cook, D. (1992). Psychosocial inpact of disability. In: R.M. Parker, E.M. Szymanski (Eds.), *Rehabilitation Counseling: Basics and Beyond* (2nd ed.), pp. 249-272. Austin, TX: Pro-ed.
Cowen, E.L., Underberg, R.P., Verillo, R.T. (1958). The development and testing of an attitudes to blindness scale. *J. Soc. Psychol.*, 48: 297-304.
Cubbage, M.E., Thomas, K.R. (1989). Freud and disability. *Rehab. Psychol.*, 34: 161-173.
Epstein, L., Feiner, A.H. (1979). Countertransference: The therapist's contribution to the treatment: An overview. *Contemp. Psychoanal.*, 15: 489-513.
Ferenczi, S., Rank, O. (1923). *The Development of Psychoanalysis*. New York: Dover Publications.
Fichten, C.S., Amsel, R. (1988). Thoughts concerning interactions between

college students who have a disability and their nondisabled peers. *Rehab. Counsel. Bul.*, 32:22-40.

Freud, A. (1936). *The Ego and the Mechanisms of Defense.* In: *The Writings of Anna Freud*, vol. 2 (rev. ed.). New York: International Universities Press, 1966.

Freud, S. (1910). The future prospects of psycho-analytic therapy. *SE*, 11, 1957, pp. 139-152.

—— (1912). Recommendations for physicians practicing psychoanalysis. *SE*, 12, 1957, pp. 109-120.

—— (1914). On narcissism: An introduction. *SE*, 14, 1957, pp. 67-102.

—— (1917). Mourning and melancholia. *SE*, 14, 1957, pp. 237-255.

—— (1924a). The economic problem of masochism. *SE*, 19, 1961, pp. 155-172.

—— (1924b). The dissolution of the Oedipus complex. *SE*, 19, 1961, pp.173-182.

—— (1926). Inhibitions, symptoms amd anxiety. *SE*, 20, 1959, pp. 87-182.

—— (1933). *New Introductory Lectures on Psychoanalysis. SE*, 22, 1964, pp. 1-182.

Gill, M. (1983). The interpersonal paradigm and the degree of the therapist's involvement. *Contemp. Psychoanal.*, 19: 202-237.

Giovacchini, P.L. (1982). *A Clinician's Guide to Reading Freud.* New York: Jason Aronson.

Gitelson, M. (1952). The emotional position of the analyst in the psycho-analytic situation. *Int. J. Psycho-Anal.*, 33: 1-10.

Glasser, B., Strauss, A. (1964). Awareness contexts and social interaction. *Amer. Sociol. Rev.*, 29: 669-679.

Grinberg, L. (1962). On a specific aspect of counter-transference due to projective identification. *Int. J. Psycho-Anal.*, 43: 436-440.

Gwyther, O.A. (1984). The psychosocial adjustment of the burn patient. In: D.W. Krueger (Ed.), *Rehabilitation Psychology: A Comprehensive Textbook.* Rockville, MD: Aspen Publications, pp. 319-327.

Heimann, P. (1950). On counter-transference. *Int. J. Psycho-Anal.*, 31: 81-84.

—— (1960). Counter-transference. *Br. J. Med. Psychol.*, 33: 9-15.

Horney, K. (1939). *New Ways in Psychoanalysis.* New York: W.W. Norton.

Huebner, R.A., Thomas, K.R. (1995). The relationship between attachment, psychopathology, and intervention for children with disabilities. *Rehab. Psychol.*, 40:111-124.

Jones, E. (1953). *The Life and Work of Sigmund Freud* (vol. 1). New York: Basic Books.

Kleck, R. (1968). Physical stigma and non-verbal cues emitted in face-to-face interaction. *Hum. Rel.*, 21: 19-28.

Kleck, R., Ono, H., Hastorf, A. (1966). The effects of physical deviance upon face-to-face interaction. *Hum. Rel.*, 19: 425-436.

Kohut, H. (1959). Introspection, empathy, and psycho-analysis. *J. Amer. Psycho-anal. Assn.*, 7: 459-483.

Kohut, H. (1979). The two analyses of Mr. Z. *Int. J. Psycho-Anal.*, 60: 3-27.
—— (1982). Introspection, empathy, and the semi-circle of mental health. *Int. J. Psycho-Anal.*, 63: 395-407.
Kohut, H., Wolf, E.S. (1978). The disorders of the self and their treatment: An outline. *Int. J. Psycho-Anal.*, 59: 413-425.
Krueger, D.W. (1981-1982). Emotional rehabilitation of the physical rehabilitation patient. *Int. J. Psychia. Med.*, 11: 183-191.
Langs, R. (1976). *The Therapeutic Interaction* (vol. 2). New York: Jason Aronson.
Little, M. (1951). Counter-transference and the patient's response to it. *Int. J. Psycho-Anal.*, 32: 32-40.
—— (1957). "R" – The analyst's total response to his patient's needs. *Int. J. Psycho-Anal.*, 38: 240-254.
—— (1960). Counter-transference. *Br. J. Med. Psychol.*, 33: 29-31.
Livneh, H. (1985). Death attitudes and their relationship to perceptions of physically disabled persons. *J. Rehab.*, 51(1): 38-41.
Lynch, R.T., Thomas, K.R. (1994). People with disabilities as victims: Changing an ill-advised paradigm. *J. Rehab.*, 60(1): 8-11.
Orr, D.W. (1955). Transference and countertransference: A historical survey. *J. Amer. Psychoanal. Assn.*, 2: 647-662.
Racker, H. (1953). A contribution to the problem of counter-transference. *Int. J. Psycho-Anal.*, 34: 313-324.
—— (1957). The meanings and uses of countertransference. *Psychoanal. Q.*, 26: 303-357.
—— (1968). *Transference and Countertransference*. New York: International Universities Press.
Reich, A. (1951). On counter-transference. *Int. J. Psycho-Anal.*, 32: 25-31.
—— (1960). Further remarks on counter-transference. *Int. J. Psycho-Anal.*, 41: 389-395.
—— (1966). Empathy and countertransference. In: A. Reich, *Psychoanalytic Contributions*. NewYork: International Universities Press, 1973.
Reich, W. (1933). *Character Analysis*. New York: Orgone Institute Press. 1945.
Rutter, M. (1981). Psychological sequelae of brain damage in children. *Amer. J. Psychia.*, 138: 1533-1544.
Sandler, J. (1976). Counter-transference and role-responsiveness. *Int. Rev. Psycho-Anal.*, 3: 43-47.
Searles, H. (1959). Oedipal love in the counter-transference. *Int. J. Psycho-Anal.*, 40: 180-190.
—— (1967). The "dedicated physician" in the field of psychotherapy and psychoanalysis. In: R. W. Gibson (Ed.), *Crosscurrents In Psychiatry and Psychoanalysis*. Philadelphia: J. B. Lippincott, pp. 128-143.
Siedel, J.D., Chadwick, O.F.D., Rutter, M. (1975). Psychological disorders in

crippled children: A comparative study of children with and without brain damage. *Develop. Med. Child Neurol.*, 17: 563-573.

Siller, J. (1984). The role ofpersonality in attitudes toward those with physical disabilities. In: C.J. Golden (Ed.), *Current Topics in Rehabilitation Psychology*. Orlando, FL: Grune & Stratton, pp. 201-227.

—— (1988). Intrapsychic aspects of attitudes toward persons with disabilities. In: H.E. Yuker (Ed.), *Attitudes Towards Persons with Disabilities*. New York: Springer, pp. 67-80.

Stolorow, R.D., Brandchaft, B., Atwood, G.E. (1987). *Psychoanalytic Treatment: An Intersubjective Approach*. Hillsdale, NJ: Analytic Press.

Stone, L. (1961). The transference-countertransference complex. In: L. Stone, *The Psychoanalytic Situation: An Examination of its Development and Essential Nature*. New York: International Universities Press, pp. 66-83.

Tauber, E. S. (1954). Exploring the therapeutic use of psychoanalytic data. *Psychia.*, 17, 331-336.

Thomas, K.R. (1994). Drive theory, self psychology, and the treatment of persons with disabilities. *Psychoanal. Psychother.*, 11: 47-55.

—— (1995). Attitudes toward disability: A phylogenetic and psychoanalytic perspective. In: J. Siller, K.R. Thomas (Eds.), *Essays and Research on Disability*. Athens, GA: Elliott & Fitzpatrick, pp. 121-128.

Thomas, K.R., Garske, G.G. (1995). Object relations theory: Implications for the personality development and treatment of persons with disabilities. *M. Klein Obj. Rel.*, 13(2): 31-63.

Thomas, K.R., McGinnis, J.D. (1991). The psychoanalytic theories of D.W. Winnicott as applied to rehabilitation. *J. Rehab.*, 57(3): 63-66.

Thompson, C. (1956). The role of the analyst's personality in therapy. *Amer. J. Psychother.*, 10: 347-359.

Tower, L.E. (1956). Countertransference. *J. Amer. Psychoanal. Assn.*, 4: 224-255.

Trieshmann, R.B. (1981). Psycho-social issues for persons with spinal cord injuries. *Paraplegic News*, 35(8): 26-31.

—— (1988). *Spinal Cord Injuries: Psychological, Social, and Vocational Rehabilitation* (2nd. ed.). New York: Demos.

Tucker, S.J. (1984). Patient-staff interaction with the spinal cord patient. In: D.W. Krueger (Ed.), *Rehabilitation Psychology: A Comprehensive Textbook*. Rockville, MD: Aspen Publications, pp. 257-266.

Turner, J.R., McLean, P.D. (1989). Physical disability and psychological distress. *Rehab. Psychol.*, 34: 225-242.

Winnicott, D.W. (1949). Hate in the counter-transference. *Int. J. Psycho-Anal.*, 30: 69-75.

—— (1960). Counter-transference. *Br. J. Med. Psychol.*, 33: 17-21.

Wolstein, B. (1983). The pluralism ofperspectives on countertransference.

Contemp. Psychoanal., 19:506-521.

Wolstein, B. (1988). Introduction. In: B. Wolstein (Ed.), *Essential Papers on Countertransference*. New York: New York University Press, pp. 1-15.

Yuker, H.E. (Ed.) (1988). *Attitudes Toward Persons with Disabilities*. New York: Springer.

University of Wisconsin
at Madison
432 N. Murray Street
Madison, WI 53706-1490
USA

JOURNAL OF MELANIE KLEIN AND OBJECT RELATIONS
Volume 15, Number 1, March 1997

WHY I HAVE NOT PREFACED
ANY OF MARCEL BÉNABOU'S BOOKS[1,2]

Warren Motte

Marcel Bénabou's *Why I Have Not Written Any of My Books* is one of the most intriguing—and most amusing—books published in France in recent years. It is *a peculiar* book (I use that term in high admiration), full of sudden twists and delightful quirks. The contrary character of its title is amply sustained throughout the book. Bénabou writes against literature in a sense, deliberately balking convention and the expectations of his reader; he proceeds, as Tweedledee might put it, "contrariwise." These effects make for refreshing, even astonishing, reading. Yet they also (and here is my caveat lector) make it extremely difficult to account for this book in a preface. For *Why I Have Not Written Any of My Books* is itself prefatory from beginning to end. Or rather, more properly, from beginning to beginning, because wherever one finds oneself in this book, it always seems to be the beginning. On the first page, Bénabou solemnly tells us that the first lines of a book are the most important ones and should be composed with the greatest of care. That which he identifies as his own "first page," however, occurs a dozen pages later; and still later there is a new beginning, which must, he says, be a very short sentence. So it goes throughout this book as one advances from threshold to threshold, running ever faster to stay in place.

In his own preface, addressed directly "To the Reader," Bénabou lists all the things he will not do in his book. He will not praise the oral at the expense of the written. He will not execrate language, or valorize the inexpressible and silence, or praise life over literature, or argue that inaction is superior to action. He swears up and down that his intent is not to destroy literature, and he assures us that in the end doubt and irony will be conquered by seriousness and faith. The contract he offers his reader is thus a contrary one; yet it is nonetheless seductive, promising as it does an appetizing dynamic of struggle, crisis, and ultimate resolution. Bénabou renews that promise in different manners again and again in *Why I Have Not Written Any of My Books*, dangling it in front of his reader's eyes playfully. The ludic quality of that gesture is, I believe, central to his project: Bénabou stages his book as a game in which an author attempts to write an impossible book, impossible because it cannot be merely a book but must rather be *the* book, something like the Book of all books. One of the principal rules of the game is that at each turn he must begin again from "go," such that every utterance be a prolegomenon, each word a foreword, in a book that is itself a preface to a far longer, definitive, perfectly embodied—and thus clearly impossible—Book. Genially and with high good humor, Bénabou invites his reader to play this game along with him, pretending that each moment in *Why I Have Not Written Any of My Books* is in fact the inaugural moment of the book.

In that very spirit, allow me to begin my review again, this time in a more conventional fashion. Marcel Bénabou was born in Meknès, Morocco. According to him, the "mythology" of his family was a proud one, looking backward over four centuries and including among its notable figures rabbis, cabalists, and miracle workers of various sorts. He mentions that in more recent times his family, though living far from France, entertained a deep interest in French culture, especially French literature, and notes that the writer Pierre Loti described a meeting with one of Bénabou's ancestors in his travel book, *Into Morocco* (1889). Bénabou himself went to study in Paris at the École Normale Supérieure, that hothouse where the most exotic flowers of the French intelligentsia take root. He earned his doctorate in Roman history at the Sorbonne and became a professor at the University of Paris VII, where he continues to teach. Despite what the title of this book suggests, Bénabou is indeed the author of a previous book, and a very learned one at that, *The African Resistance to Romanization* (1976). *Why I Have Not Written Any of My Books* was published in 1986, and it won a distinguished French literary award, the Black Humor Prize. Two books in much the same ironic vein follow upon it, *Throw This Book Away Before It's Too Late* (1992) and *Jacob, Menachem, and Mimoun: A Family Epic* (1995).

In April 1969 Marcel Bénabou joined the Ouvroir de Littérature Potentielle [Workshop of Potential Literature], or "Oulipo" for short. Founded in 1960 by Raymond Queneau and François Le Lionnais, the Oulipo is a group of writers and mathematicians interested in problems of literary form. That interest is double: on the one hand, they are devoted to the identification and rehabilitation of old, even ancient, forms, such as the triolet or the lipogram; on the other hand, they propose to elaborate new ones, often (but not always) based on mathematical structures. The Oulipo's membership would come to include figures such as Marcel Duchamp, Italo Calvino, Jacques Roubaud, and Harry Mathews. It was Bénabou's longtime friend Georges Perec, the author of *Life: A User's Manual* and *W or The Memory of Childhood*, and in many ways the quintessential Oulipian, who introduced Bénabou to the group. He threw himself into the Oulipo's work with enthusiasm, collaborating with Perec on a project entitled "Automatic Production of French Literature" (a game much like word golf, but using whole words for pawns, rather than letters), composing

"antonymical" poetry (in which each word in a poem is replaced by its ant-
onym), experimenting with the combinatoric potential of proverbs and apho-
risms. During the last twenty-five years, Bénabou has participated assiduously
in the Oulipo's public activities as well (readings, colloquia, writers workshops),
and the group has in turn gratified him with the official title Definitively
Provisional Secretary.

If I dwell here on the Oulipo, it is because of the tremendous influence it
exerted on Bénabou as a writer. That influence can be read, I think, on every
page of *Why I Have Not Written Any of My Books*. The ludic spirit that animates
the text is largely Oulipian in inspiration, suggesting as it does that playfulness
and seriousness of purpose are not mutually exclusive. Like his fellow
Oulipians, Bénabou is closely, constantly attentive to form. He plays joyfully on
the shape of words, just as he does on the shape of the book, encoding for
example names of writers (Edmond Jabès, Perec, and, on a couple of occasions,
"Bénabou") homophonically in his text. A good deal of Bénabou's play is
organized mathematically, in fine Oulipian fashion, though the techniques of
formal constraint underlying that organization are studiously discreet, verging
on the clandestine. The number three recurs insistently in the structure of the
text. There are three sections, each containing three further divisions, the first
and last paragraphs contain three sentences, and so forth. Bénabou uses three
types of discourse: narrative, dialogue, and "borrowed" language (quotation,
allusion, pastiche); each major theme is treated thrice, once in each discursive
mode. Appearances notwithstanding, *Why I Have Not Written Any of My Books*
is in fact a highly constructed piece of work. Bénabou plays tradition and
innovation against each other in a manner that proves their reciprocal comple-
mentarity; there is an astonishing literary erudition at work here, all the more
surprising in a book that pretends to be unlike any other book. Finally, the
notion that the ideal "Book" exists only as a hypothetical construct in a *potential*
state, always waiting to be written, owes at least as much to the Oulipo's
theories of potential literature as it does to Mallarmé.

That notion serves as the very motor of *Why I Have Not Written Any of My
Books*. It is a source of much of the humor in the text, as Bénabou pursues the
Book, chasing it as it flees maddeningly before him. He knows it's out there, he
sees it, he has suspected its existence ever since he learned to read, but— damn
it all!—he just can't *write* it. His own text at times becomes a meditation on im-
possibility, as he enumerates, with maniacal attention to detail, the reasons why
he cannot write the Book. He argues that one should not attempt to write before
one is fully mature. Yet he realizes, with despair, that it is *always* either too early
to write— because one's too young, too callow—or too late, because others
(Stendhal! Flaubert! Proust! Sartre!) have already constructed such formidable
literary monuments. Faced with the classic modernist alternative of writing or
living, he finds himself incapable of either, and chooses to adopt a sort of

tortured quietism. That choice is amply reflected in the style of *Why I Have Not Written Any of My Books*, for Bénabou's prose is deliberately tortured. His sentences in the original are involuted and laborious; exceptionally long, they strain on the page. David Kornacker [the English translator] has rendered these effects with wonderful fidelity; yet such effects, a source of great fun for Bénabou's reader, must certainly have posed great challenges for his translator.

Bénabou's style, then, illustrates the principal axiom of his book, that writing is torture and, practically speaking, impossible. For Bénabou, at least, if not for others. And there is the rub: Why have others succeeded where he encounters only failure and desperation? Those "others," both canonical figures and contemporaries, loom ominously throughout the book. Bénabou quotes them or alludes to them continually, comparing his writing to theirs and always coming up short. The first of these intertextual gestures is contained in his title, which plays on Raymond Roussel's *How I Wrote Certain of My Books* (1935). The reference is apt and highly charged with irony, for Roussel's book possesses what is surely one of the most misleading titles in literary history. Purporting to explain such hermetic masterpieces as *Impressions of Africa* and *Locus Solus*, *How I Wrote Certain of My Books* in fact does nothing of the sort. It is, rather, a reflection on writing itself, on its modes and conditions of possibility. Bénabou suggests that his own title may be read as "a provocation" and compares his allusion to Roussel to the paradox of the Cretan liar. Taking both provocation and paradox into account, the reference to Roussel in the title helps Bénabou position his book for the reader in two important ways. First, it allows him to declare that his book will not be a conventional one; it is not "about" anything other than writing. Second, it serves to inscribe the book—both ironically and straightforwardly—under the sign of Roussel himself, perhaps the most exemplary *writer's writer* of French modernism and foremost in a long line of Bénabou's "others."

Other "others"quickly follow. Epigraphs abound in this book as Bénabou quotes directly from Julien Benda, Novalis, Jorge Luis Borges, Maurice Blanchot, Ecclesiastes, Miguel de Unamuno, Walter Benjamin, E. M. Cioran, Maimonides, Nicholas de Chamfort, Simone de Beauvoir, René Char, Jules Renard, Lichtenberg, "Mallursset" (a conflation of Mallarmé and Musset), Jean Paulhan, Pierre Reverdy, Jacques Derrida, Pascal, J. Vicens, and Maurice de Guérin. He alludes, explicitly or more obliquely, to Shakespeare (in a rollicking parody of Shylock's speech from Act 3 of *The Merchant of Venice*), to Racine, Diderot, Chateaubriand, Hölderlin, Novalis, Stendhal, Poe, Hugo, Flaubert, Henri Amiel, Nietzsche, Rimbaud, Mallarmé, Proust, Gide, Antonin Artaud, Pierre Jean Jouve, Michel Leiris, Sartre, Jabès, and Perec. Other people's writing plays a huge role in the textual economy of *Why I Have Not Written Any of My Books*, and Bénabou muses ironically upon that fact: do those references serve to render his own writing palatable, or is his own writing merely a pretext for these exercises in erudition? Among many other considerations, one appears to be salient: these precursors said "it" better (or at least said it first). And they are, to a man—*pacet* Beauvoir—writer's writers, just the sort of writer Bénabou aspires to be.

In this vast field of reference, some things stand out. Granted the auto-diegetical character of his project, Bénabou compares his book implicitly to certain canonical "confessional" texts like Stendhal's *Life of Henri Brulard*, Gide's *If It Die*, Leiris's *Manhood*, and Sartre's *Words*, finding these comparisons distinctly unflattering, to say the least. Three figures in particular hover exasperatingly over *Why I Have Not Written Any of My Books*. First Flaubert: if the author of *Madame Bovary* once claimed to "be" Emma Bovary, so, too, does Bénabou. For he experiences literature like an affliction, from within, so that it becomes his only reality, and an unlivable one at that. His rereading of Flaubert's novel convinces him that his paltry efforts at writing are futile. Bénabou's book is moreover quite patently a *Sentimental Education*, a novel of apprenticeship that mocks that very genre, where irony anticipates irony and the benighted protagonist learns, in effect, nothing. Proust, too, strides mightily through these pages. And inevitably so: how can a writer named "Marcel" undertake to write about things past without being compared to Proust? And how can this "Marcel" dare to rival that one? Finally, Bénabou's friend Georges Perec appears frequently in this book. Bénabou plays on Perec's name, refers to him as a "master," alludes lovingly to his writings (most notably in a pastiche of the beginning of Perec's first novel, *Things*). Perec's *W or The Memory of Childhood*, like *Sentimental Education*, like *Remembrance of Things Past*, offers a model of writing that Bénabou recognizes as nearly perfect and for that very reason impossible to emulate. If only he, like Borges's Pierre Menard with the *Quixote*, could rewrite those books and call them his own! But of course that won't work either.

Daunted by the writing that surrounds him, Bénabou focuses his haggard gaze on the writing within. Each sentence, each word he writes reminds him that he is, in fact, *writing*; and each sentence in turn shouts that declaration out from the page. *Why I Have Not Written Any of My Books* is a funhouse (to use John Barth's term), a hall of mirrors where the writing subject and the subject of writing are infinitely and comically reflected, to the point of hallucination. The effect of textual specularity, the notion of the book-as-chronicle-of-its-own-elaboration, has been a key feature of contemporary French literature since Gide's *The Counterfeiters* (1925). In recent years, that topos has become in a sense the imposed figure of "serious" writing, in the absence of which no text can aspire to distinction. In its maturity, then, the topos becomes ripe for parody, and Bénabou plays roundly and gleefully upon the notion of the specular text. Explaining with quite alarming insincerity that his book will not exploit facile "specular games," Bénabou intends in fact that his book should *exhaust* the possibilities of writing on writing, exhausting through that same exaggerative gesture the specular text as genre. For never was a book as utterly—and drolly —devoted to itself as *Why I Have Not Written Any of My Books*.

Bénabou also plays on the important (and currently much-vexed) issue of confessional writing, in the same disingenuous spirit. He assures his reader that autobiography and confessional literature in general interest him not one whit. Yet his book is focused squarely on the catastrophic dilemma of *him*-self: though be was "born to write" (everyone in his circle, family and friends, always quite naturally assumed that he would become a writer), he in fact cannot write. He speaks of how his vocation declared itself during his childhood in Meknès: just as the Jews were the chosen of God, so too he was the chosen of literature. Writing for him was more than a desire; it was an idée fixe. He tells of how he tried to write later in life, during his vacations in the French countryside. Having assembled all his writing utensils, his voluminous notes, his earlier aborted texts, he stares at the empty paper before him: no inspiration comes, and in no vacation spot does he succeed in writing "his" books. The very *paper* resists him, for God's sake, and this despite the fact that he has erected a veritable cult around it.

He is always buying paper or taking it from others, hoarding it against the day when he'll need it, reams and reams of it. Indeed Bénabou is an accomplice in the paper's resistance: its white purity awes him, and he does everything to conserve it. In short, as he tries to conquer that which he always thought he legitimately *possessed*, literature, he is reduced—like Job, like Portnoy—to a long, resounding wail.

In his torment, a new idea occurs to him. Does not having written a book perhaps suffice, in itself, to distinguish a man? Despite their ultimate vanity, might his arduous labors make him a hero? The mythological heroes he evokes—Sisyphus, Penelope, Tantalus, the Danaides—are, after all, heroic precisely by virtue of the fact that they labor uselessly, they wait, they yearn, they are beset; and they bear their torment nobly. Such a vision of the heroic fits in nicely with a more contemporary game Bénabou plays, that of "loser wins," a familiar gambit of the avant-garde. If the role of the hero as traditionally conceived is unsuitable (too conventional, too confining, or perhaps on the contrary too demanding), perhaps one can be an antihero. Or even a schlemiel, which is the role Bénabou takes on when he describes himself as an "irresolute hero, a Hamlet of the library." The image is an apt one, all the more so in that it points to the real conflict that subtends Bénabou's relations with literature, a conflict between being and doing; though he has always felt that he is a writer, what he has always done is to read literature rather than write it. He speaks of his readerly bulimia as an apprenticeship; in his mind, he was always reading in order eventually to write. But the writing, alas, never came.

Which brings me to my new beginning and to the only question that makes any sense here: Why has Marcel Bénabou not written any of his books? Bénabou

poses that question incessantly, addressing his readers directly and immediately, as kindred spirits, assuming that we understand and sympathize with
him. And we do, we do! But what are we reading, after all? He tells us twice,
echoing Diderot and Magritte and shamelessly indulging his taste for paradox,
ceci n'est pas un livre; although he admits that it might closely resemble a book,
he still maintains that it is a "non-book." But—Hell's bells!— let's get real here.
It *is* a book. Hath it not a binding? Hath it not pages, parts, introduction,
conclusion? If you spill coffee on it, does it not stain? If you lend it to your
brother-in-law, shall he not fail to return it? If you assign it to your undergradu-
ates, shall they not neglect to read the preface?

NOTES

1. Oftentimes we came across books which are not "directly" related to analysis,
   feeling that somehow this is a plus for both our readers and for us. Bénabou's book
   is such a book: original, challenging and thought provoking. Many thanks to Meg
   Childland (New York) who brought this book to our attention. (Ed.)
2. Reprinted from *Why I Have Not Written Any of My Books* by Marcel Bénabou by
   permission of the University of Nebraska Press. © 1996 by the University of
   Nebraska Press.

University of Colorado   JOURNAL OF MELANIE KLEIN AND OBJECT RELATIONS
at Boulder   **Volume 15, Number 1, March 1997**
Campus Box 238
Boulder CO 80309
USA

Change of Address?

If you are anticipating a change of address, please notify us as soon as possible to
ensure uninterrupted delivery of your issues.

Send change of address to:

JMKOR, 1 Marine Midland Plaza

East Tower – Fourth Floor

Binghamton, New York 13901-3216 USA

International Institute of Object Relations Therapy

IIORT

Study with Leading Voices in Object Relations
in Washington, DC with

Anne Alvarez
▼
Salman Akhtar
▼
Christopher Bollas
▼
Earl Hopper
▼
Gregorio Kohon
▼
Stanley Ruszcynski
▼
Neville Symington
▼
A. Hyatt Williams
▼
Isca Wittenberg

Object Relations Theory and Practice
➤ One and two year certificate programs in individual, couple and family therapy
➤ Annual institutes in couple and family therapy
➤ Object relations weekend conferences
➤ Directed by DAVID and JILL SCHARFF

NATIONAL PROGRAMS in Washington DC Metro Area
with distinguished guests and IIORT Faculty

LOCAL STUDY GROUPS AND COURSES in Charlottesville, Chevy Chase, Long Island,
Manhattan, Omaha, Philadelphia, Salt Lake, San Diego and Panama

For more information, call us at 301-215-7377,
or e-mail IIORT@mindspring.com

NOTES ON CONTRIBUTORS

MAURICE APPREY, Ph.D. is Professor of Psychiatric Medicine and Associate Dean, University of Virginia School of Medicine. With Howard Stein he is the co-author of the three volume series, *Ethnicity, Medicine, and Psychoanalysis* (University Press of Virginia) and *Intersubjectivity, Projective Identification, and Otherness* (Duquesne University Press). He is the English language translator of Gerorge Politzer's *Critique of the Foundations of Psychology: The Psychology of Psychoanalysis* (Duquesne University Press).

Mrs. MEG HARRIS WILLIAMS, M. Litt. (Oxon) is a writer, artist, and teacher at the University of Surrey. She is the author of papers, book chapters, and books. Her forthcoming book, *A Trial of Faith* is to be published by Karnac Books, London.

PATRICK MAHONY, Ph.D. is Training and Supervising Analyst, Canadian Psychoanalytic Society; full professor, Université de Montreal; Fellow of the Royal Society of Canada; author of *Freud as a Writer* (1987), *On Defining Freud's Discourse* (1989), *Freud and the Rat Man* (1986), *Les Pleurrs de l'Homme aux Loupes* (1995), *Psychoanalysis and Discourse* (1986), *Freud's Dora: A Psychoanalytical, Historical, and Textual Study* (1996); principal co-editor of *Freud in Correspondence* (1997).

DONALD MELTZER, M.D. is a psychoanalyst in private practice in Oxford, England. He is the author of *The Psycho-Analytical Process* (1967), *Sexual States of Mind* (1973), principal author of *Explorations in Autism* (1975), *The Kleinian Development* (1978), *La comprensione della belezza e altri saggi di psicoanalisi* (1981), *Dream Life* (1984), *Studies in Extended Metapsychology* (1986), principal author of *The Apprehension of Beauty* (1988), *The Claustrum* (1992), and *Sincerity and Other Works* (1994).

WARREN MOTTE, Ph.D. is Professor of French and Comparative Literature at the University of Colorado at Boulder. His most recent publications include *Literary Ludics* (Ed.) (1991), *Alteratives* (Co-Ed.) (1993), *Playtexts: Ludics in Contemporary Literature* (1995). He has published over 80 articles and book reviews.

MICHAEL IAN PAUL, M.D. is Assistant Clinical Professor of Psychiatry at UCLA School of Medicine, and Training and Supervising Analyst at the Los Angeles Psychoanalytic Institute, and the Psychoanalytic Center of California. He is presently working on a volume of psychoanalytic phenomenology of primitive mental states to be published this summer. He is in private practice in Beverly Hills, California.

Mr. ERIC RHODE is a psychoanalytic psychotherapist in private practice in London, England. He is a Visiting Teacher at the Children and Families Department, the Tavistock Clinic, and a Training Therapist with the Association for Group and Individual Psychotherapy and the London Centre for Psychotherapy. His publications include *On Birth and Madness* (1987), *The Generations of Adam* (1990), and *Psychotic Metaphysics* (1994). He has recently finished *On Hallucination, Intuition, and the Becoming of "O"*, to be published this year.

KENNETH R. THOMAS, D.Ed., is Professor, Department of Rehabilitation Psychology and Special Education, School of Education, University of Wisconsin-Madison. He is the author of many articles, book chapters and book reviews.

Mr. ROBERT T. WASKA, M.S., M.F.C.C. is a psychoanalytic psychotherapist in private practice in San Francisco, CA, and candidate at the San Francisco Institute for Psychoanalytic Psychotherapy and Psychoanalysis.

CALL FOR BOOK AND FILM REVIEWS

The *Journal of Melanie Klein and Object Relations* is accepting book and film reviews, and reviews of several books in the form of essays. Send manuscripts to the Book Review Editor. All manuscripts should conform to the style of this publication (see "Instructions for Authors" in this issue, pp. 175-

BOOKS RECEIVED

Association Française de Psychiatrie (1991). *W.R. Bion, une théorie pour l'avenir.* Paris: Métailié, 166 pp.

Bach, F.T., Rowell, M., Temkin, A. (1995). *Constantin Brancusi. 1876-1957.* Philadelphia Museum of Art, 406 pp. (Book received courtesy of Meg Childland, New York.)

Bénabou, M. (1996). *Why I Have not Written Any of My Books.* Translated by D. Kornacker. Preface by W. Motte. Lincoln and London: University of Nebraska Press, 112 pp. (Book received courtesy of Meg Childland, New York.)

Bion, W.R. (1983). *Seminari italiani.* Translated by Parthenope Talamo Bion and Laura Rachele Piperno. Roma: Edizioni Borla, 132 pp. (Ital.)

Bion, W.R. (1993), *Ganduri secunde. Lucrari selectate de psihanaliza. (Second Thoughts. Selected Papers on Psycho-Analysis.)* Translated by F. V. Vladescu, C. Bujdei and C. Braga. Introductory study by J. S. Grotstein. Binghamton and Cluj: *esf* Publishers, 234 pp. (Romanian)

Bion, W.R. (1994). *Seminarii braziliene.* (Brazilian Lectures.) Translated by V. Stanciu. Edited by F. V. Vladescu. Binghamton and Cluj: *esf* Publishers, 190 pp. (Romanian)

Boris, H. (1993). *Passions of Mind. Unheard Melodies: A Third Principle of Mental Functioning.* New York: New Yok University Press.

Boris, H. (1994). *Envy.* Northvale and London: Jason Aronson, 200 pp.

Boris, H. (1994). *Sleights of Mind. One and Multiple of One.* Northvale and London: Jason Aronson, 364 pp.

Cicchetti, D., Nurcombe, B. (Eds.) (1996), *Development and Psychopathology.* Special issue: *Regulatory Processes,* 8(1), 306 pp. (Journal issue received courtesy of Meg Childland, NYC.)

Fischer-Schreiber, I., Ehrhard, F-K., Friedrichs, K., Diener, M.S. (1994). *The Encyclopedia of Eastern Philisophy and Religion.* Boston: Shambhala, 468 pp.

Freud, S. *Oeuvres complètes. Psychanalyse.* Vol. III: 1894-1899 (1989). Translated by J. Altounian, A. Bourguignon, P. Cotet, R. Doron, F.-M. Gathelier, H. Hildebrand, J. Laplanche, A. Lindenberg, A. Rauzy, J. Stute-Cadiot. Paris: Presses Universitaires de France, 308 pp. (Fren.)

Freud, S., *Oeuvres complètes. Psychanalyse.* Vol. X: 1909-1910 (1993). Translated by J. Altounian, A. Balseinte, A. Bourguignon, P. Cotet, R. Lainé, A. Rauzy, J. Stute-Cadiot, E. Wolff. Paris: Presses Universitaires de France, 340 pp. (Fren.)

Freud, S., *Oeuvres complètes. Psychanalyse.* Vol. XIII: 1914-1915 (1988). Translated by J. Altounian, A. Balseinte, A. Bourguignon, A. Cherki, P. Cotet, J.-G.

Delarbre, D. Hartman, J.-R. Ladmiral, J. Laplanche, J.-L. Martin, A. Rauzy, Ph. Spulez. Paris: Presses Universitaires de France, 350 pp. (Fren.)

Freud, S., *Oeuvres complètes. Psychanalyse*. Vol. XVI: 1921-1923 (1991). Translated by J. Altounian, C. Avignon, C. Baliteau, I. Biesinger, A. Bloch, A. Bourguignon, B. Chabot, P. Cotet, J.-G. Delarbre, J. Doron, R. Doron, F.-M. Gathelier, D. Hartman, R. Lainé, J. Laplanche, A. Rauzy, F. Robert, J.-M. Rondeau, F. Stute-Cadiot. Paris: Presses Universitaires de France, 426 pp. (Fren.)

Freud, S., *Oeuvres complètes. Psychanalyse*. Vol. XVII: 1923-1925 (1992). Translated by J. Altounian, C. Avignon, A. Balseinte, A. Bourguignon, M. Candelier, C. Chiland, P. Cotet, J.-G. Delarbre, J. Doron, R. Doron, M. Hanus, D. Hartman, H. Hildebrand, R. Lainé, J. Laplanche, A. Lindberg, C. von Petersdorff, M. Pollack-Cornillot, A. Rauzy, M. Strauss. Paris: Presses Universitaires de France, 336 pp. (Fren.)

Hinshelwood, R.D. (1995). *Dictionarul psihanalizei kleiniene. (Dictionary of Kleinian Thought.)* Translated by B. Orasanu and F. V. Vladescu. Edited and introduced by F. V. Vladescu. Binghamton and Cluj: *esf* Publishers, 456 pp. (Romanian)

Klein, M. (1994). *Iubire, vinovatie si reparatie si alte lucrari: 1921-1945 (Love, Guilt, and Reparation, and Other Works: 1921-1945)*. Vol. I. Translated by L. Pavel, E. Tamaianu and F.V. Vladescu. Introduction by H. Segal. Edited by F.V. Vladescu. Binghamton and Cluj: *esf* Publishers, 414 pp. (Romanian.)

Klein, M. (1994). *Povestea unei analize de copil. (Narrative of a Child Analysis)*. Vol. IV. Translated by C. Popovici. Edited by F.V. Vladescu. Binghamton and Cluj: esf Publishers, 494 pp. (Romanian)

Manguel, A. (1996). *A History of Reading*. New York: Viking, 372 pp. (Book received courtesy of Meg Childland, NYC.)

Neri, C., Correale, A., Fadda, P. (Eds.) (1987). *Letture bioniane*. Roma: Edizioni Borla, 484 pp. (Ital.)

Ogden, T.H. (1996). *Limita primitiva a experientei (The Primitive Edge of Experience)*. Translated by D. Bucerzan and F.V. Vladescu. Edited by F.V. Vladescu. Binghamton and Cluj: *esf* Publishers, 168 pp. (Romanian)

Reppen, J. (Ed.). *Psychoanalytic Books. A Quarterly Journal of Reviews*, 1996, 7 (3), 158 pp. (Journal issue received courtesy of Francesca Reppen.)

Rhode, E. (1987). *On Birth and Madness*. London: Duckworth, 222 pp. (Book received courtesy of the author.)

Rhode, E. (1990). *The Generations of Adam*. London: Free Association Books, 158 pp. (Book received courtesy of the author.)

List your book here . . .

All publishers and authors have to do is to send their books to us. . .

INSTRUCTIONS TO AUTHORS

MANUSCRIPTS should be sent to: Prof. O. Weininger, PhD, Editor, Department of Applied Psychology, The Ontario Institute for Studies in Education, 252 Bloor Street West, Toronto, Ontario M5S 1V6, Canada.

MANUSCRIPTS should be typewritten double-spaced, including quotations and references, with one-inch margin on all sides. Send a clearly marked, PC or MAC (high density) diskette of the manuscript accompanied by two printouts on white paper. Provide an abstract of maximum 250 words, and a brief biographical note with the author(s) degree, title, affiliation, and mailing address.

THE EDITORIAL COMMITTEE welcomes manuscripts which contribute to our understanding of object relations. The length of the paper is usually determined by the content. This may include, for example, critical analyses of concepts, literature reviews leading to creative proposals, empirical research, and historical analyses. The manuscripts may be either theoretical or practical and applied. Notes about cases and treatment procedures, ideas concerning theory, and book and film reviews are invited as well. The highest ethical and professional standards must be observed in protecting the confidentiality of patients, families and groups.

TEXT DOCUMENTATION: Titles of books should be in *italics*, while titles of articles and book chapters in double quotation marks: "..." All notes should be endnotes only with clear and consecutive superscript numbering in the text of the paper. Notes and references should conform to the style in this issue of the publication. References in the text should provide the author name, and in parentheses, the year of the publication of the paper or book. *Example*: Klein (1945) wrote.... If the author's name is not included in the sentence of the text, place in parentheses the author's name, followed by a comma and the year of the publication. *Example*: The focus of my contribution is on... the emotional mathematician (Bion, 1965). For two or more publications, use semicolons to separate the names of authors. *Example*: I have later discovered that the term has been used by others (Kant, 1789; Heidegger, 1931; Wittgenstein, 1933-1935). Whenever material is quoted in the text, cite a page reference, in parentheses, at the end of the quotation. *Example*: If it went... could not endure it and must perish (p. 586).

REFERENCES should be arranged alphabetically by author. References from the same author should be listed in chronological order, beginning with the earliest source. If there are several papers by the same author, type after the first reference a double em line ———. Names of journals should be in *italics* and abbreviated as in the *Index Medicus*, or in this issue of the publication. Names of books should be in *italics*. For S. Freud's works, indicate the volume number and the pages of the paper from the *Standard Edition*. *Example*: Freud, S. (1915). Observations on transference love. *SE*, 12: 157-172. However, the first reference to a paper or book by S. Freud from the *Standard Edition* should indicate the editor's name and the complete title of the edition. *Example*: Freud, S. (1915). On beginning the treatment. *SE*, 12:123-144. In: J. Strachey (Ed.), *Standard Edition of the Complete Psychological Works of Sigmund Freud*, 24 volumes. London: Hogarth Press and The Institute of Psycho-Analysis, 1953-1974. Authors using a different edition or their own translations, should indicate so.

ILLUSTRATIONS AND COPYRIGHTS: All illustratios should be sent in black and white, camera-ready format only. If the illustration is not in camera-ready format, the authors will be billed for the costs incurred by the publisher. The authors of papers published in this journal agree to indemnify this journal and its publisher against any expenses, damages or losses resulting from the use by the author of any unauthorized photographs, words, names, sketches, illustrations (but not limited to) protected by copyright or trademark. Authors are solely responsible for the opinions and views expressed in their papers and do not necessarily reflect the viewpoints of the editor, editorial committee or the publisher.

A COMPLIMENTARY COPY of the issue in which the paper appears and a REPRINT ORDER FORM will be sent to the author(s).
